JUBILEUM

ALESSANDRA D'URSO

JUBILEUM

TEXT BY
ALESSANDRA BORGHESE

STEIDL

INTRODUCTION

Jubileum is an artistic reportage of the historic Jubilee celebration declared by Pope Francis, which began on 8 December 2015 with the opening of the Holy Door at St. Peter's Basilica in Rome.

It is curious to note that the celebration of the Jubilee originates from Jewish tradition. A holy year was observed every fifty years and tradition dictated that it be a fallow year so the land could rest and subsequent harvests would be more prosperous. To smooth over inequalities among the children of Israel, land was also returned to its owners and slaves were freed as part of the celebration. The beginning of the Jubilee was announced by the sounding of a ram's horn, known as a *yobel* in Hebrew, hence the Christian term Jubilee.

Pope Boniface VIII announced the first Jubilee in Catholic history in 1300. The event had much more spiritual significance than the Jewish holy year. Plenary indulgences for the remission of sins were promised to all those who travelled to Rome to celebrate their faith and relationship with God.

The faithful were then presented with a real tour de force: thirty visits to the Basilicas of St. Peter and St. Paul for Romans, and fifteen visits for pilgrims from outside the city. That first Jubilee was mentioned by Dante Alighieri in *The Divine Comedy* with a poetic description of the vast crowds of pilgrims at Ponte Sant'Angelo, where a two-way system was implemented to ease the traffic en route to St. Peter's Basilica – keeping to the right to enter and to the left to exit.

In 1517, Luther's Protestant Reformation was founded on criticism of this trade in indulgences. By then Pope Leo X was offering an indulgence to anybody who made a donation towards the construction of St. Peter's Basilica, without the need to travel to Rome.

Over the centuries, the interval between Jubilees changed. Today it is set at twenty-five years; the last ordinary Jubilee was held in 2000 under Pope John Paul II, and the next will be held in 2025. However, the pontiffs who rule over the Roman Church can also announce extraordinary Jubilees and this is the case for the Jubilee called by Pope

Francis on the theme of mercy. *The Seven Works of Mercy* is one of Caravaggio's most popular artworks, created between 1606 and 1607 and kept at the church of Pio Monte della Misericordia in Naples. According to the Gospel of Matthew, these are the seven tasks that Jesus asks of the faithful in order to have their sins forgiven and gain access to Paradise: feed the hungry, refresh the thirsty, dress the naked, shelter the homeless, visit the sick, visit the imprisoned, and bury the dead.

In these hard, dark and confused times of ours, where so many of the things we take for granted are threatened by war, poverty, abuse and fundamentalism, even a small act of love can make a difference. It is not just the Church but the world itself that is starved for mercy. Mercy is not specific to any faith or culture, and can offer a middle ground even amidst our differences.

Perhaps this was the motive for the Pope's choice of theme – one month before the beginning of the Jubilee he declared that "This is the time for mercy." It was no coincidence that one of the most important events of the Holy Year was the canonisation of Mother Teresa of Calcutta – a small nun who offered dignity to those most in need, the poor abandoned in the suburbs of Calcutta for whom nobody else would even spare a glance.

Sadly, the climate of this Jubilee was overshadowed by the ever-present threat and fear of the terrorist attacks that have besieged the Western world. There was constant military presence outside the basilicas and airport security measures were implemented with metal detectors and body searches of the pilgrims queuing to enter. Despite this, millions of pilgrims still made their way to Rome.

Jubileum focuses on the various events that took place on St. Peter's Square and around it. Many different things were happening all at once and the choice of what to photograph was entirely personal. Our knowledge of the city guided us over the months, along with a desire to show not only the grandiose celebrations at the Vatican, but also small, authentic gestures of faith. Pilgrimage is one of the symbols of the Jubilee: it represents a new path, a point of departure, a process of change.

From a historical perspective, Rome will always be the holy city of Catholicism. The pilgrims that come to Rome for the Jubilee are seeking absolution and profound intimacy, but also the great historic and artistic wealth of the Eternal City. There is in fact an inevitable dramaturgy that ties together Italian culture, dare I say Roman, and Catholicism.

Hence *Jubileum* can be considered a reportage that seeks to document moments and situations that are all part of a great history.

Alessandra d'Urso's photographs capture certain timeless atmospheres; some show surprising geometric detailing or an architectural play of light, others are extremely precise, and yet others eternalise human expressions and the most simple of gestures. They are powerful and poetic images that pull us into both the opulence of the Vatican and the day-to-day life of the different communities that came together in Rome during that special year which ended on 20 November 2016. These photographs are the very soul of this book and they guide us from one situation to the next, helping us to meditate and rest our minds so we can each enjoy our own personal experience of the Jubilee.

Alessandra Borghese

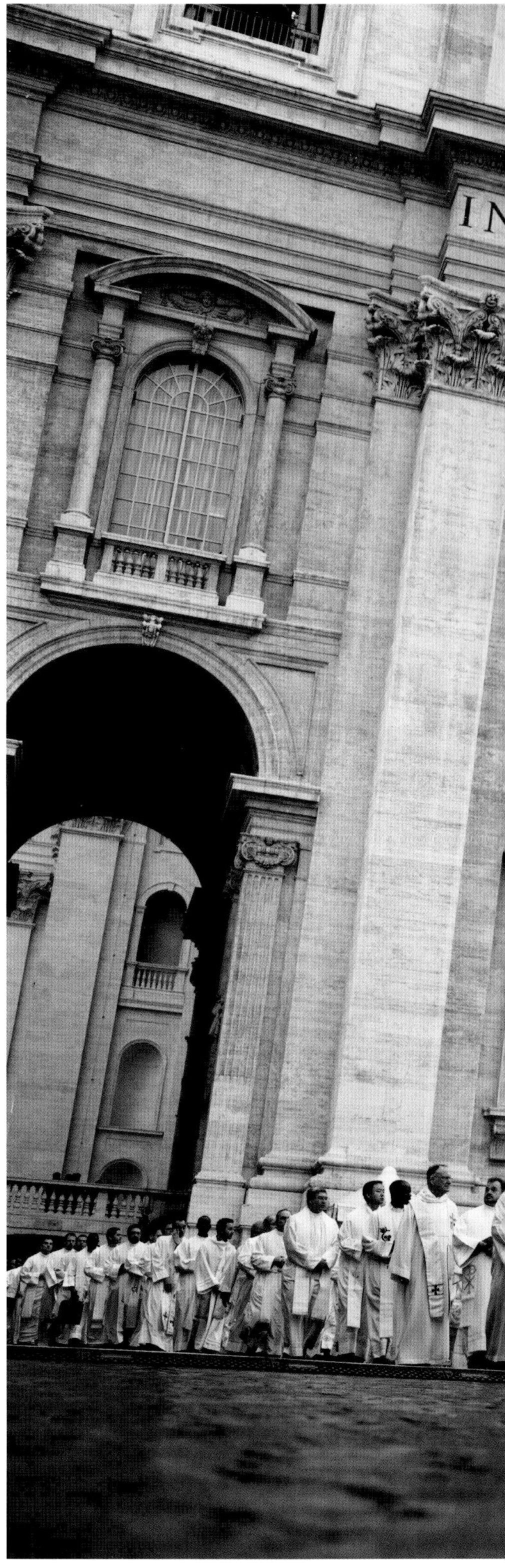

It is 8 am on 8 December 2015 and preparations for the opening celebrations of the Jubilee year are beginning. Hundreds of priests emerge in procession from St. Peter's Basilica. The piazza is crowded with pilgrims. Only the Vatican could welcome and organise so many thousands of people; the choreography is impressive.

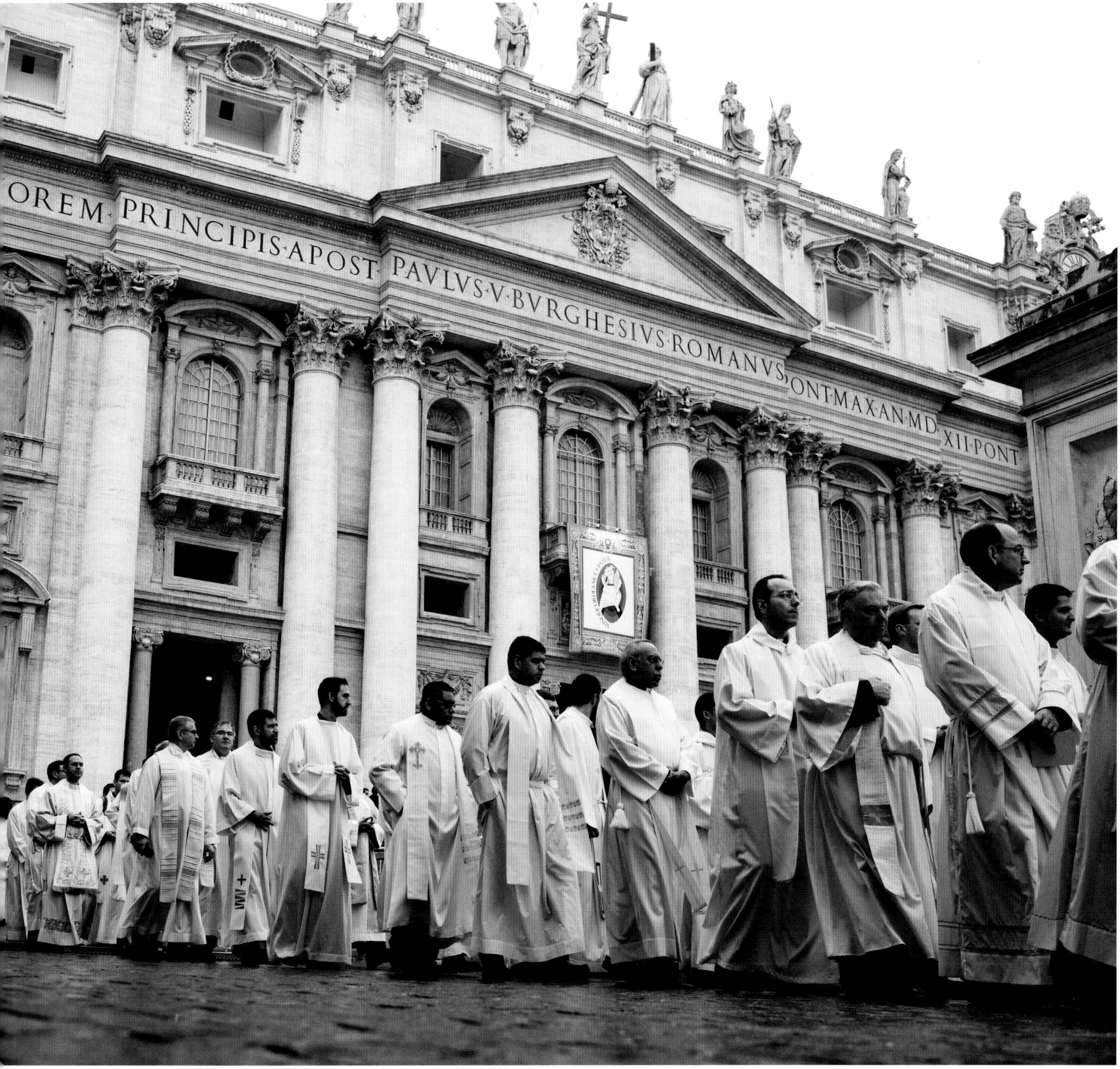
OREM·PRINCIPIS·APOST·
PAVLVS·V·BVRGHESIVS·ROMANVS
PONT·MAX·AN·MD
XII·PONT

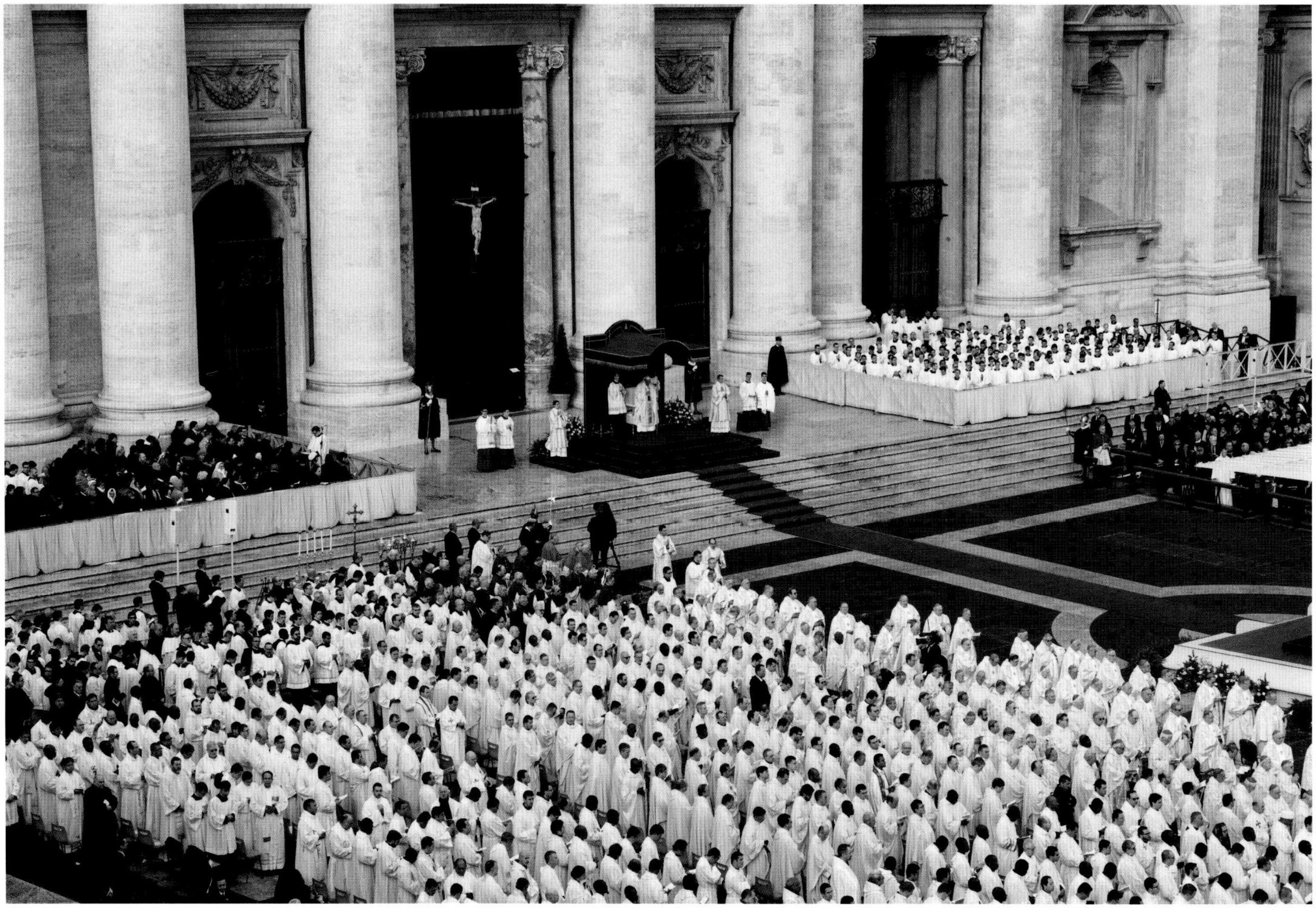

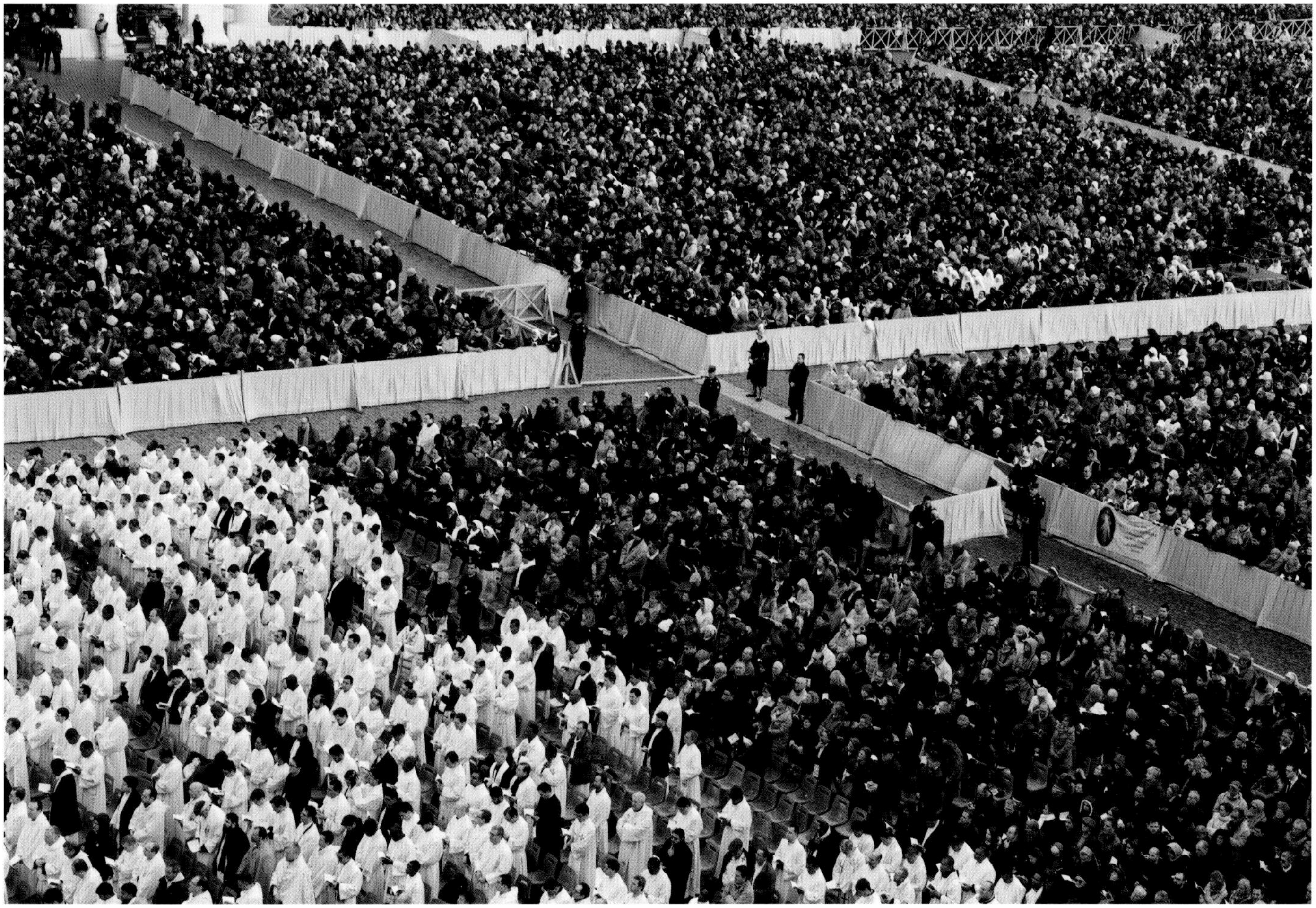

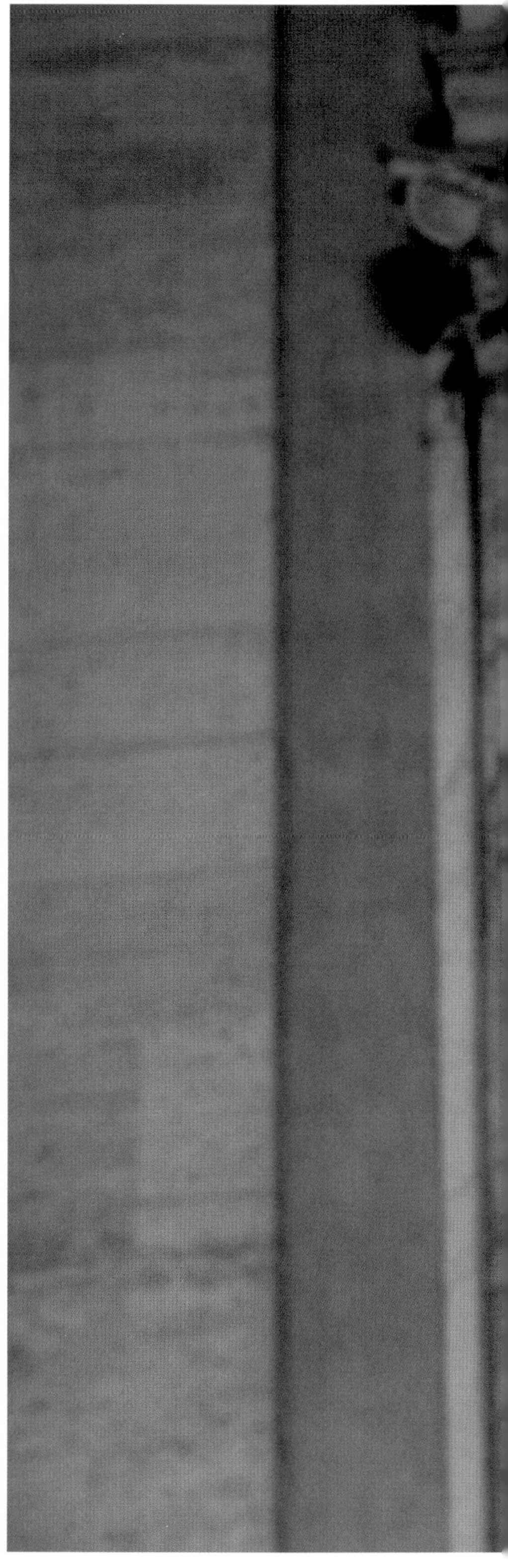

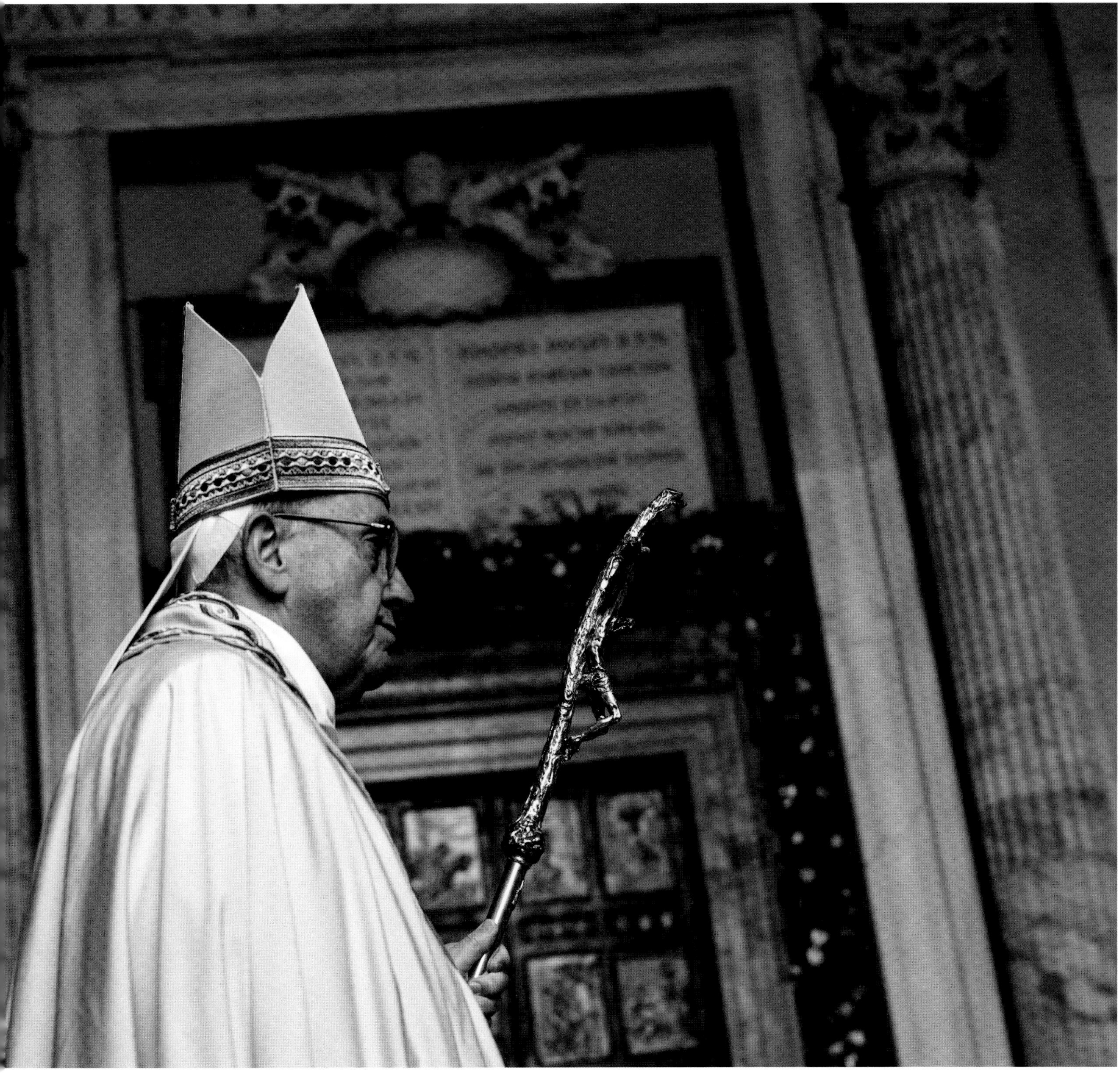

Pope Francis prepares to open the Holy Door of St. Peter's Basilica. He rests his hands on the imposing bronze door that has been closed since 2000, ready to open it wide. The rite used to be far more complicated: the pontiff had to strike the door three times with a hammer to break through the concrete that sealed it. The door represents the freedom and responsibility of all believers to cross that threshold and enter a renewed life of faith.

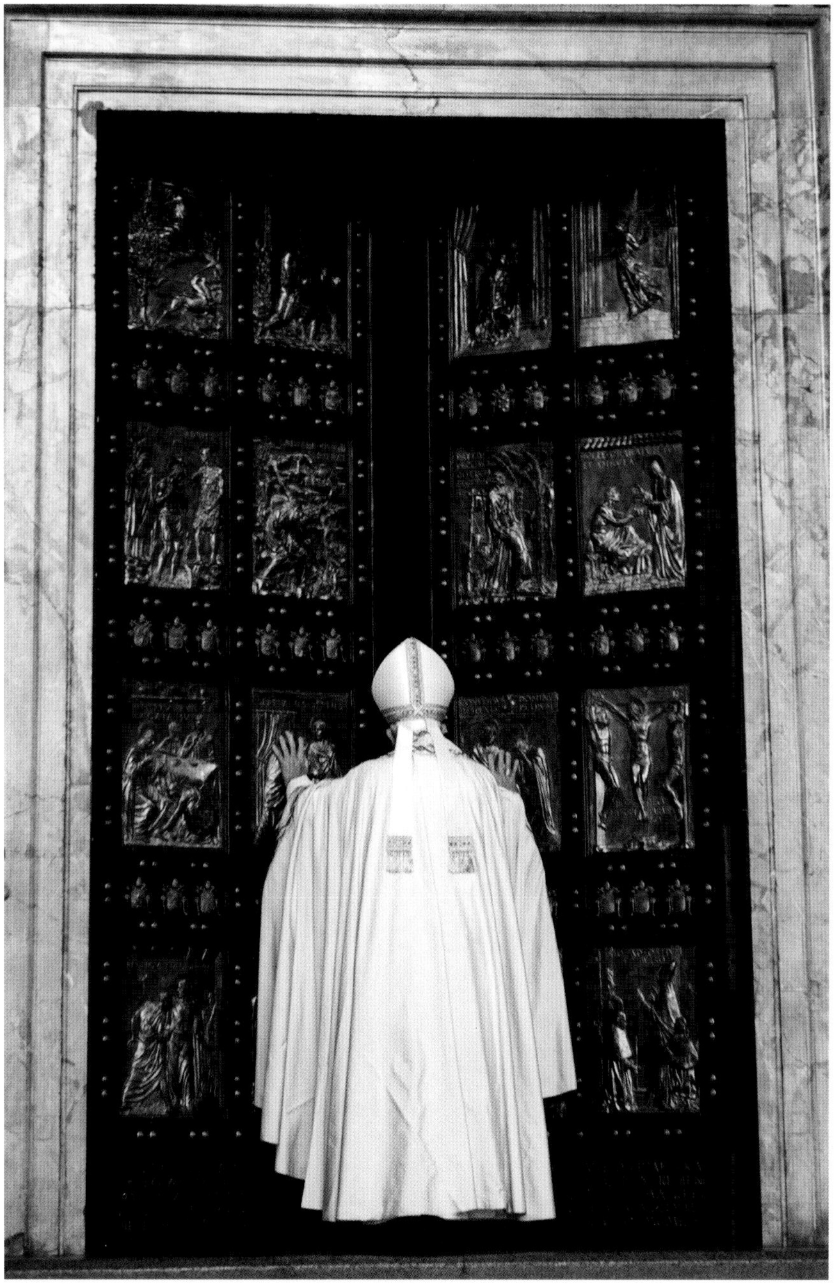

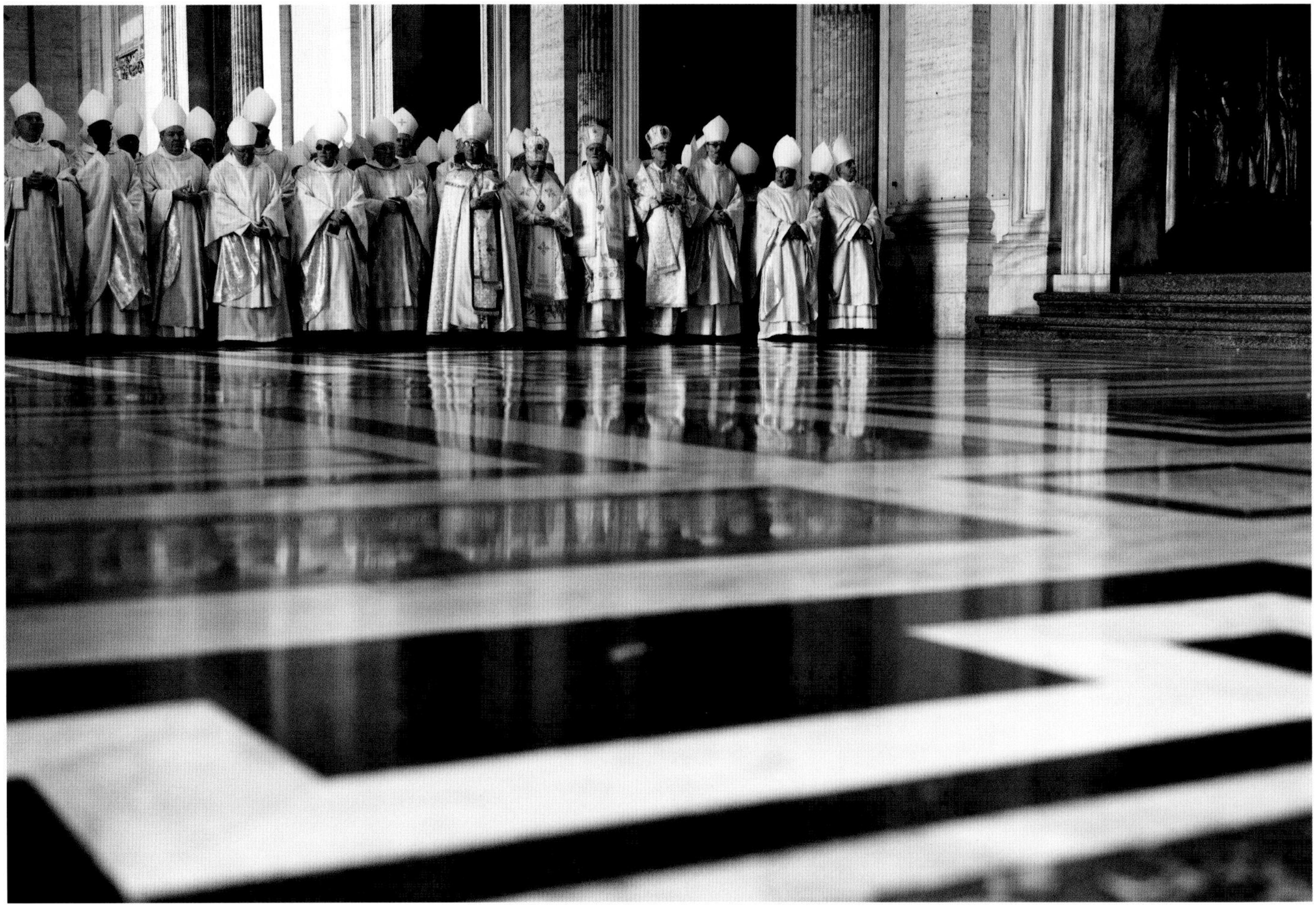

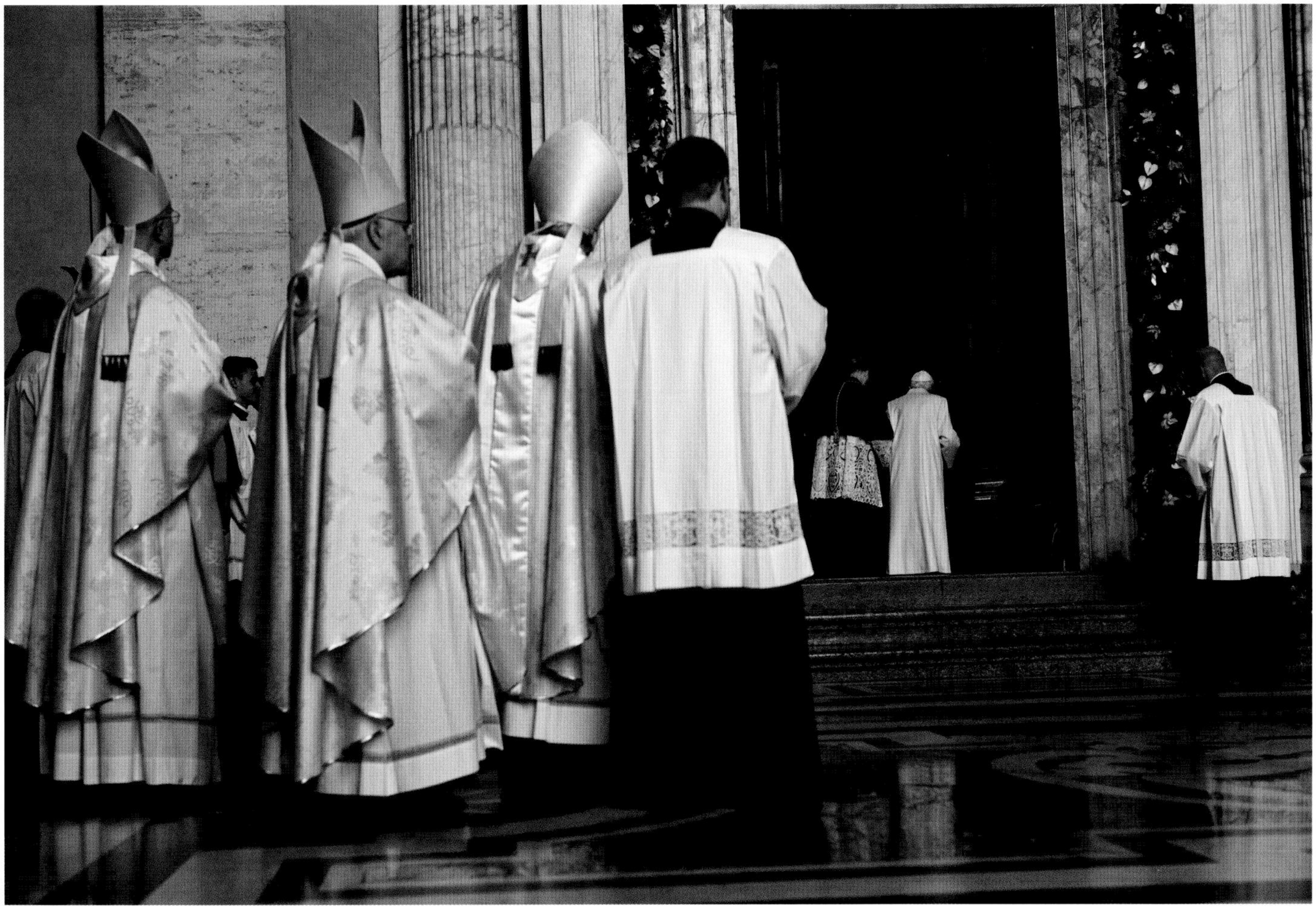

Pages 16-19

After Pope Francis, the first pilgrim to cross the threshold of the Holy Door was Pope Benedict XVI, followed by a procession of cardinals and bishops. This scenario is unique in the history of the Church. Since 11 February 2013, when Pope Ratzinger stepped down, the two pontiffs have lived just a few hundred metres from each other in the Vatican City, although only one rules over the Church. They often meet and celebrate mass together.

Pages 20-21

Every pilgrim who approaches the Holy Door has a different reaction. Some touch the door in adoration and hope, others kneel without raising their gaze; some cry while others still take photographs. The Catholic religion states that crossing the Holy Door is itself not enough to receive the indulgence. Pilgrims must also confess, receive communion, pray for the intentions of the Pope and perform an act of penitence or charity. The Jubilee is an occasion to renew one's faith and promise of devotion to Jesus Christ.

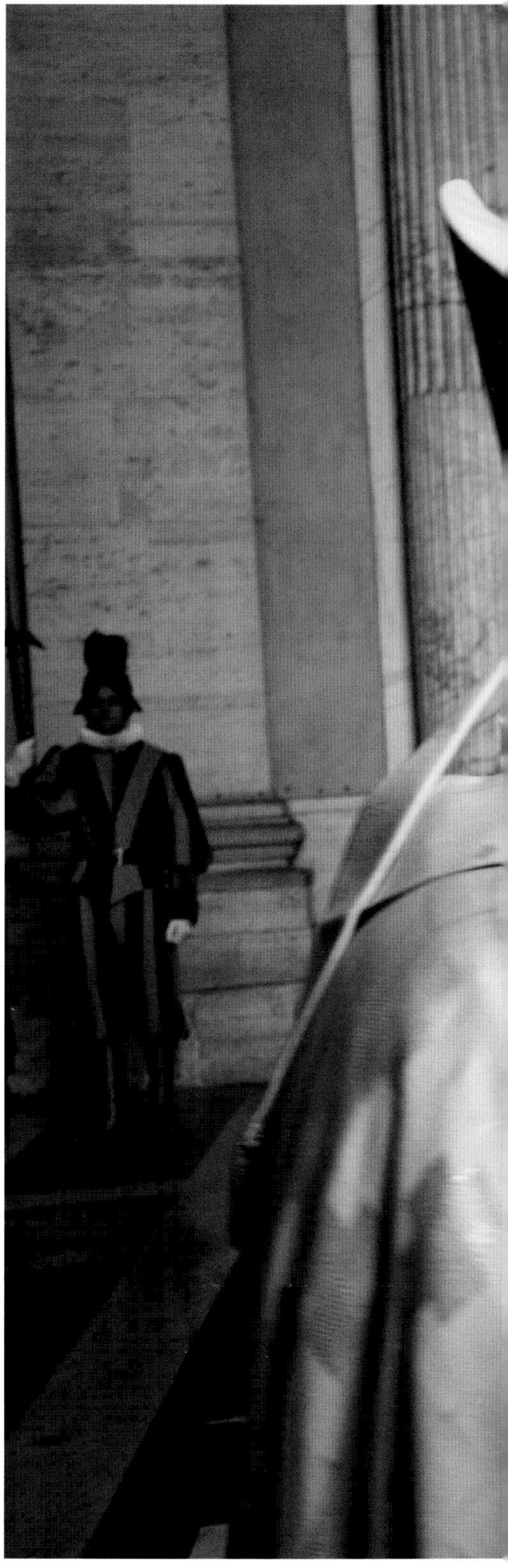

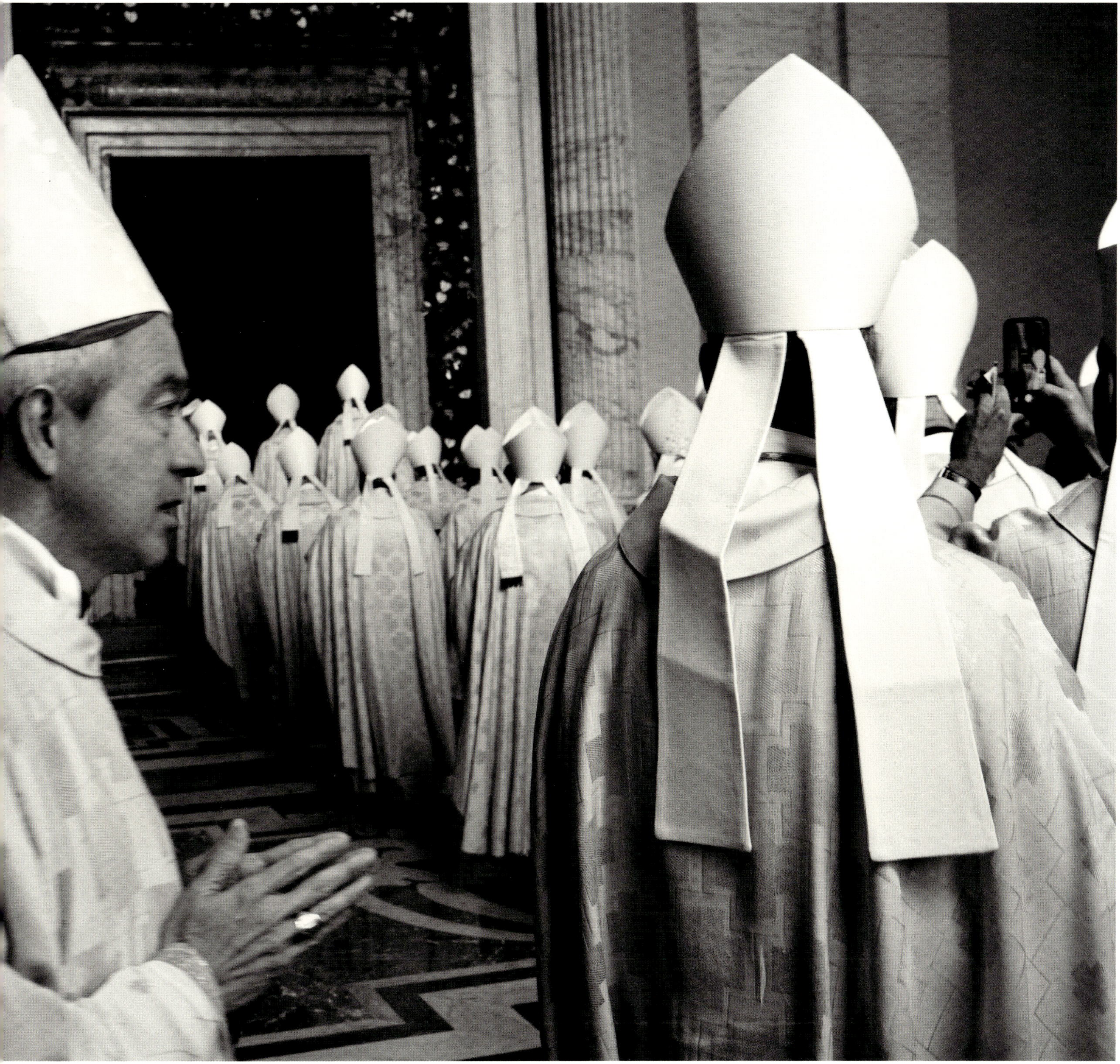

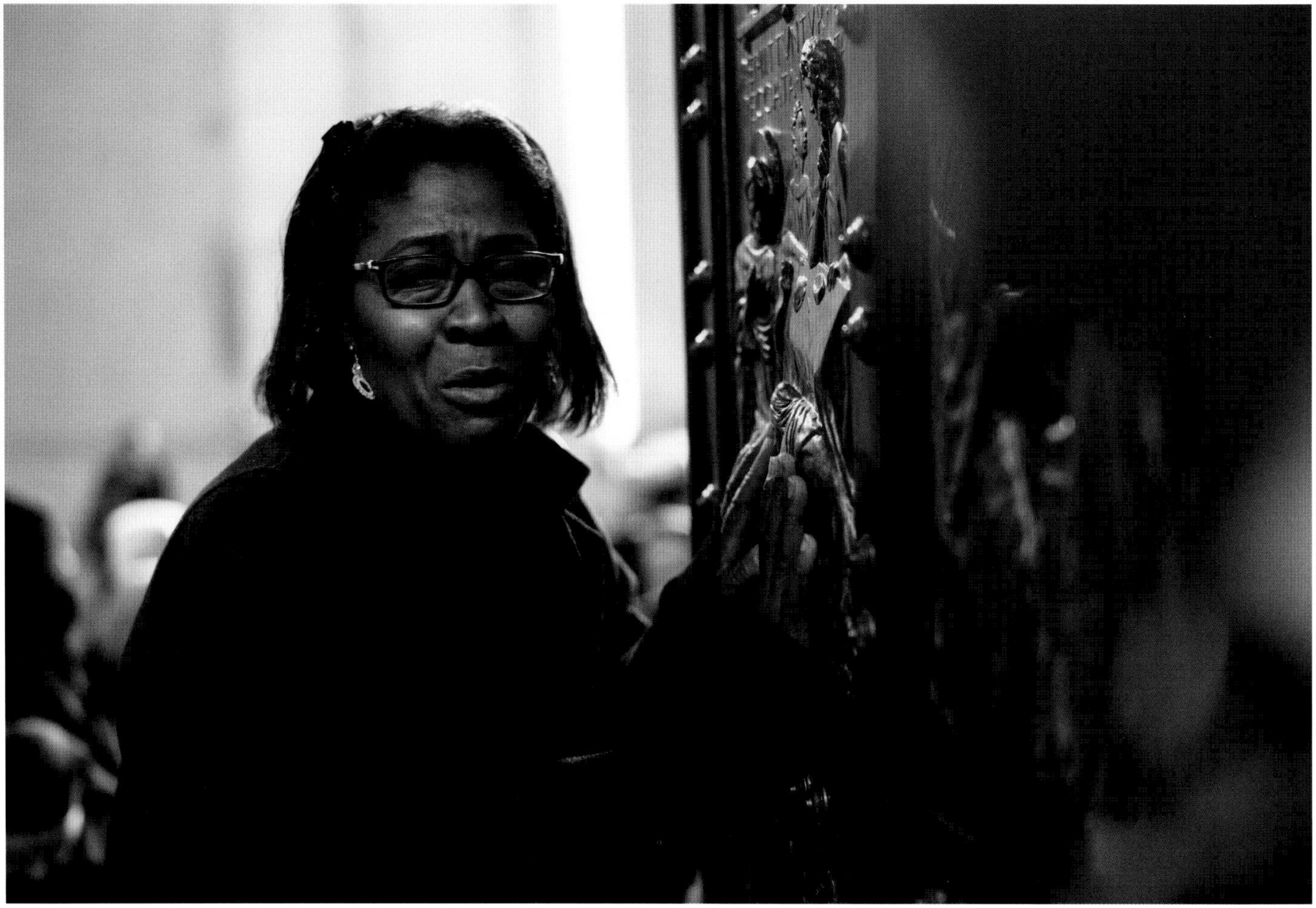

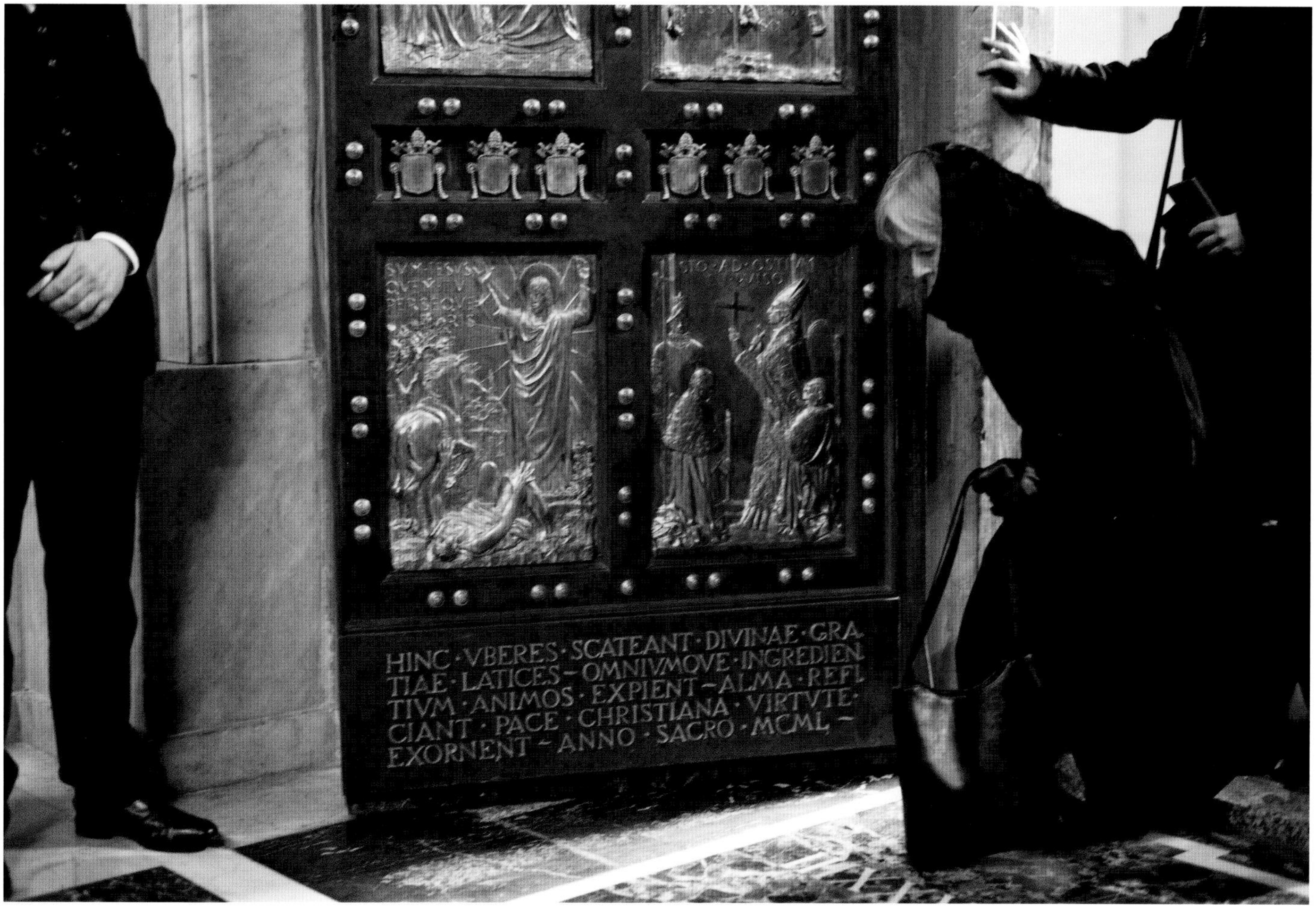
HINC · VBERES · SCATEANT · DIVINAE · GRA
TIAE · LATICES – OMNIVMQVE · INGREDIEN
TIVM · ANIMOS · EXPIENT – ALMA · REFI
CIANT · PACE · CHRISTIANA · VIRTVTE ·
EXORNENT – ANNO · SACRO · MCML –

Under Counter-Reformation guidelines, Carlo Maderno completed the facade, narthex and three bays at St. Peter's Basilica in 1600, altering the original design by Michelangelo. The church was transformed "into an instrument for mass worship" (it remains so today), and the impact of the dome on the piazza was diminished.

Pages 24-25

Inside St. Peter's Basilica, a young cleric kisses the feet of a crucifix with great spiritual devotion. It was placed there for veneration at the beginning of the Jubilee. This wooden crucifix was crafted by traditional Roman artisans and was commissioned in 2003 by the Office for the Liturgical Celebrations of the Supreme Pontiff to celebrate the twenty-fifth year of Pope John Paul II's papacy.

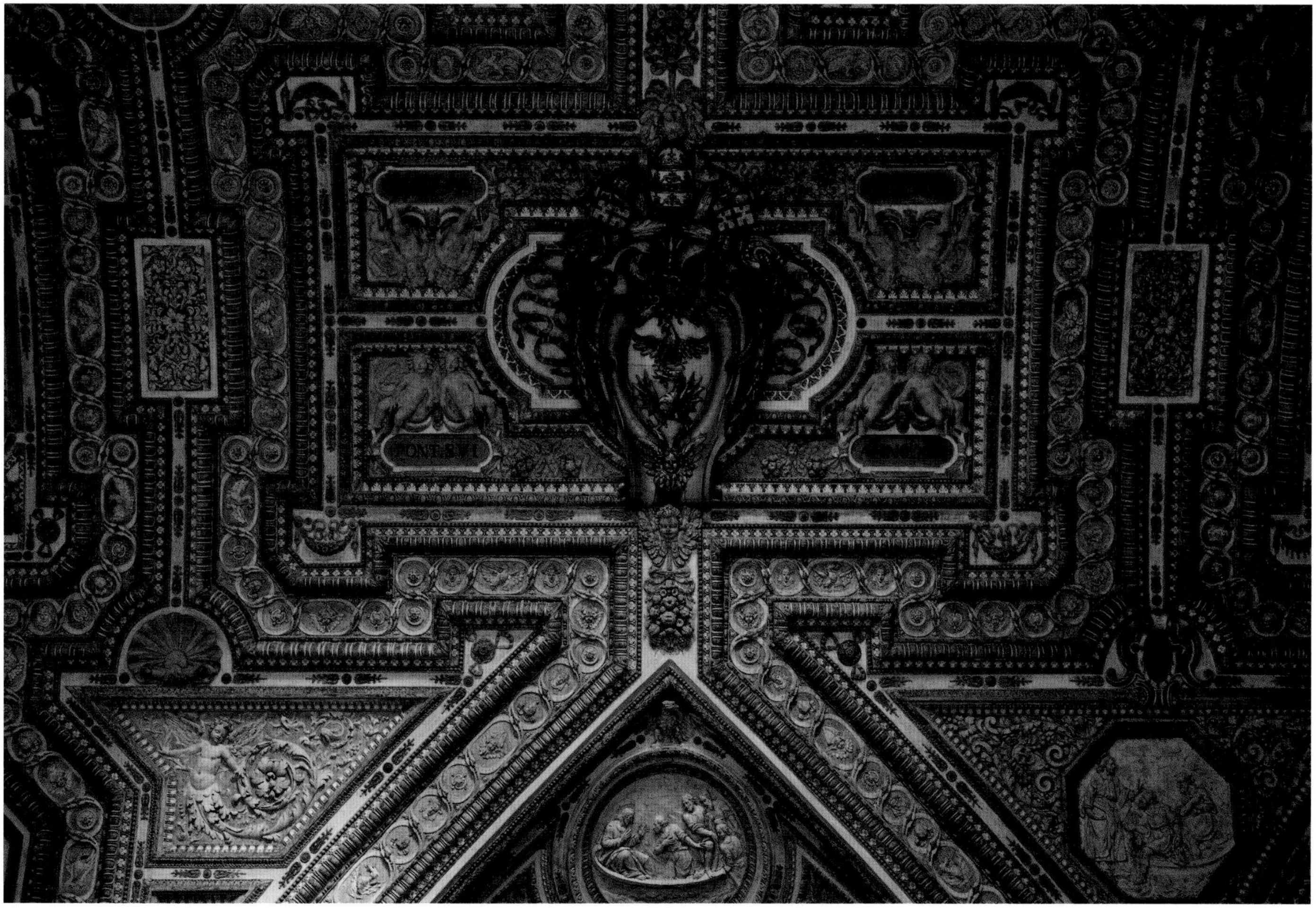

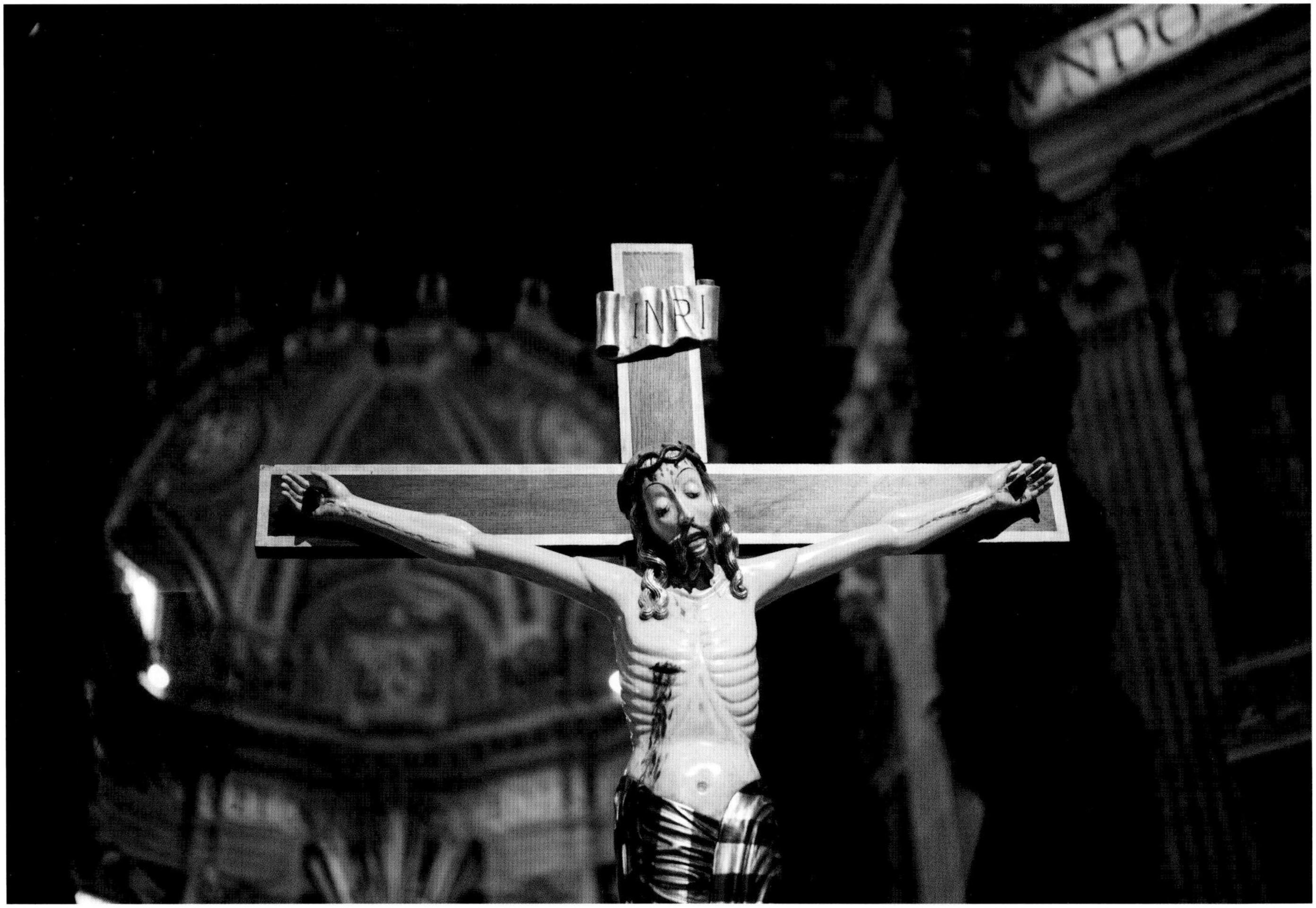
INRI

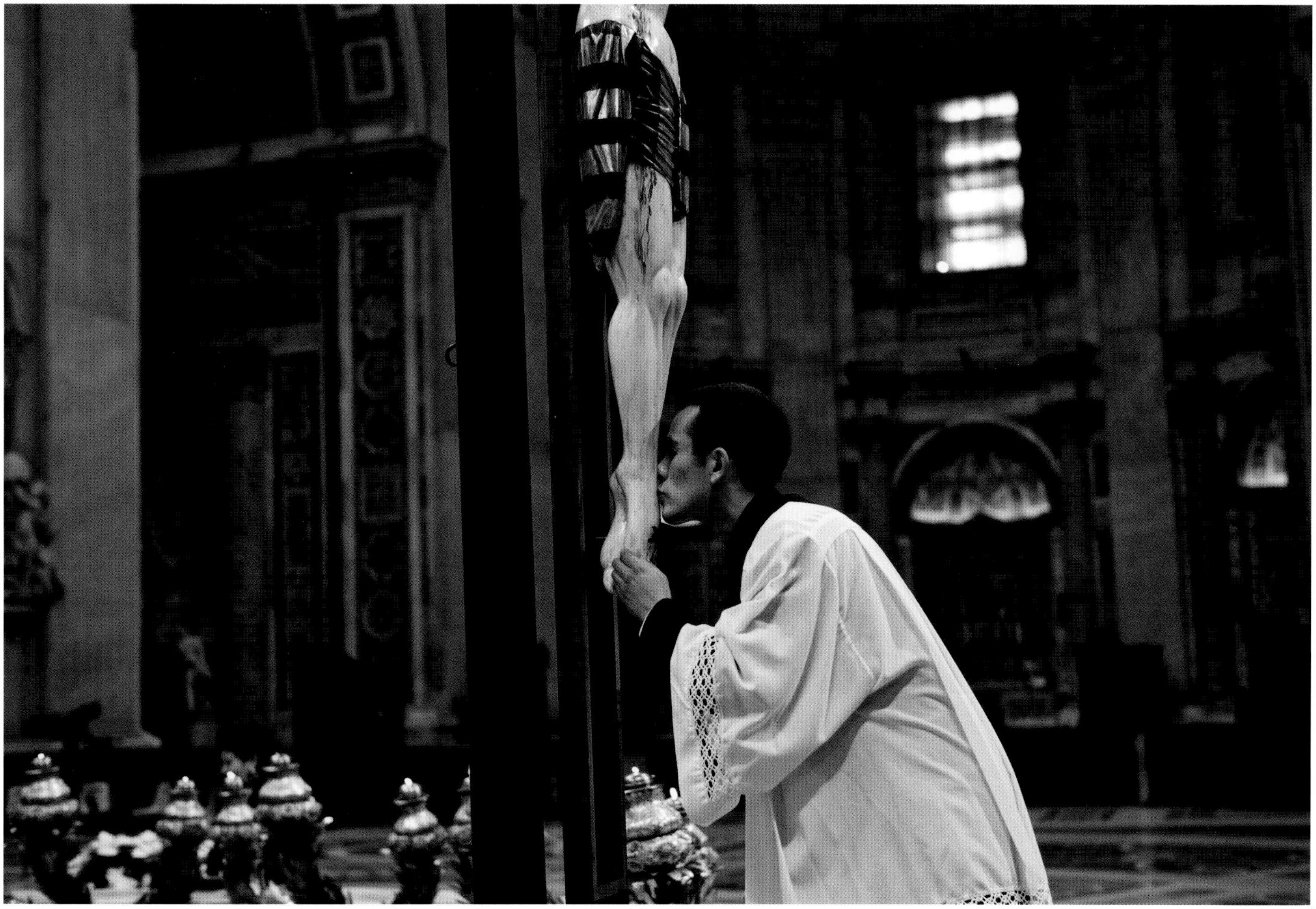

Two figures pass each other on the marble floor of St. Peter's Basilica in the turmoil after the opening ceremony.

Pages 28-29

On 1 January 2016, the World Day of Peace, Pope Francis opened the Holy Door of the Papal Basilica of Santa Maria Maggiore. This is the most beautiful church dedicated to Our Lady in the world and inside is the statue of Regina Pacis, commissioned by Pope Benedict XV to give thanks for the end of the First World War. Romans say that the face of this Virgin Mary is shrouded in sadness.

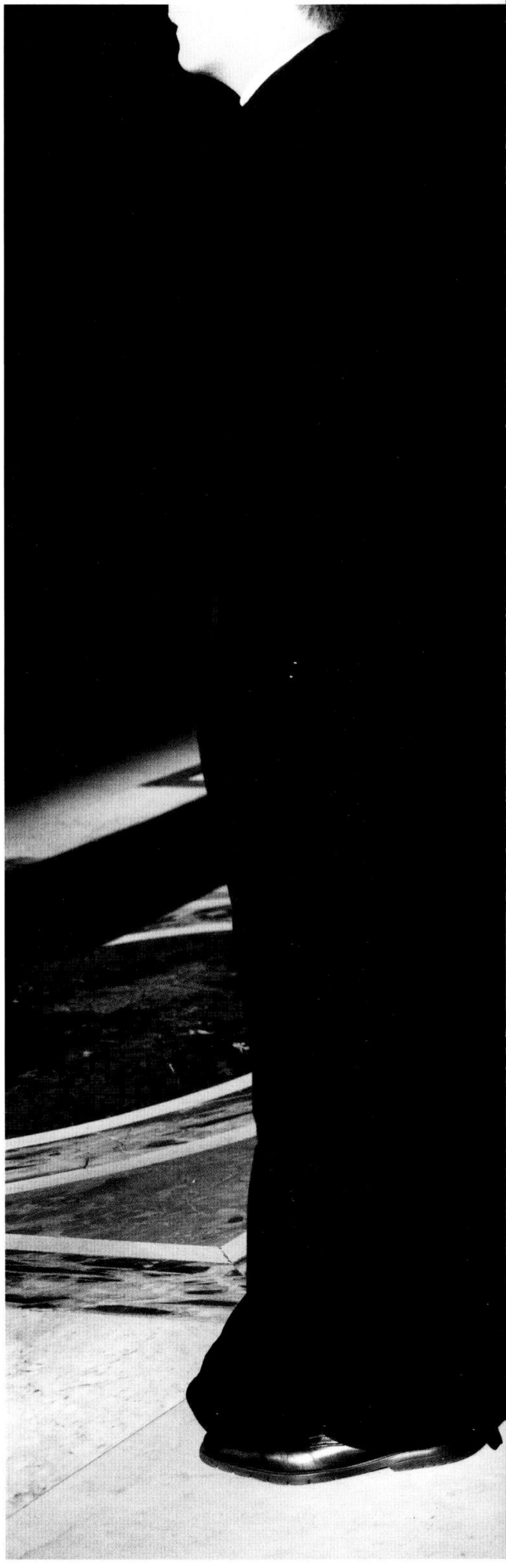

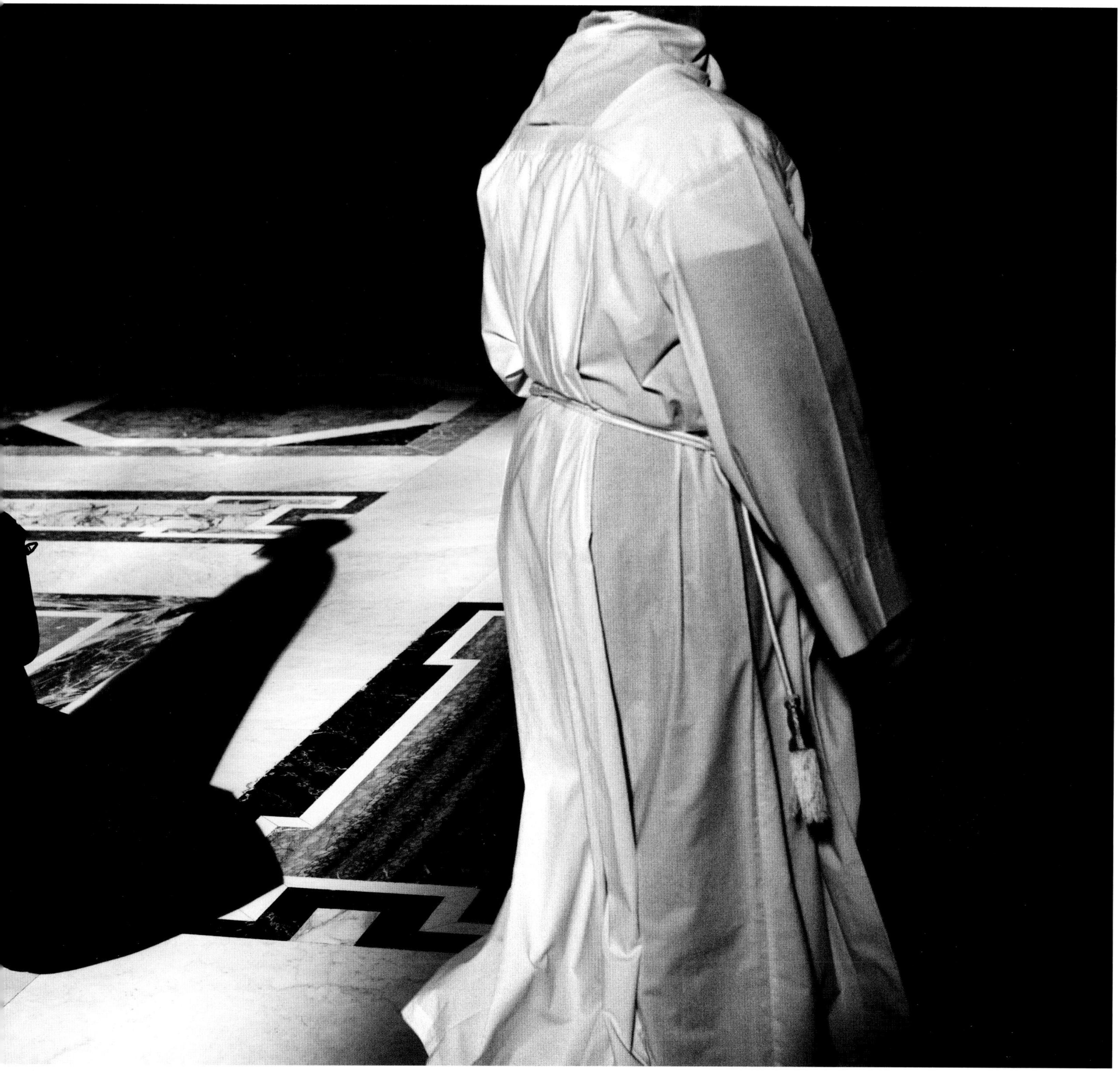

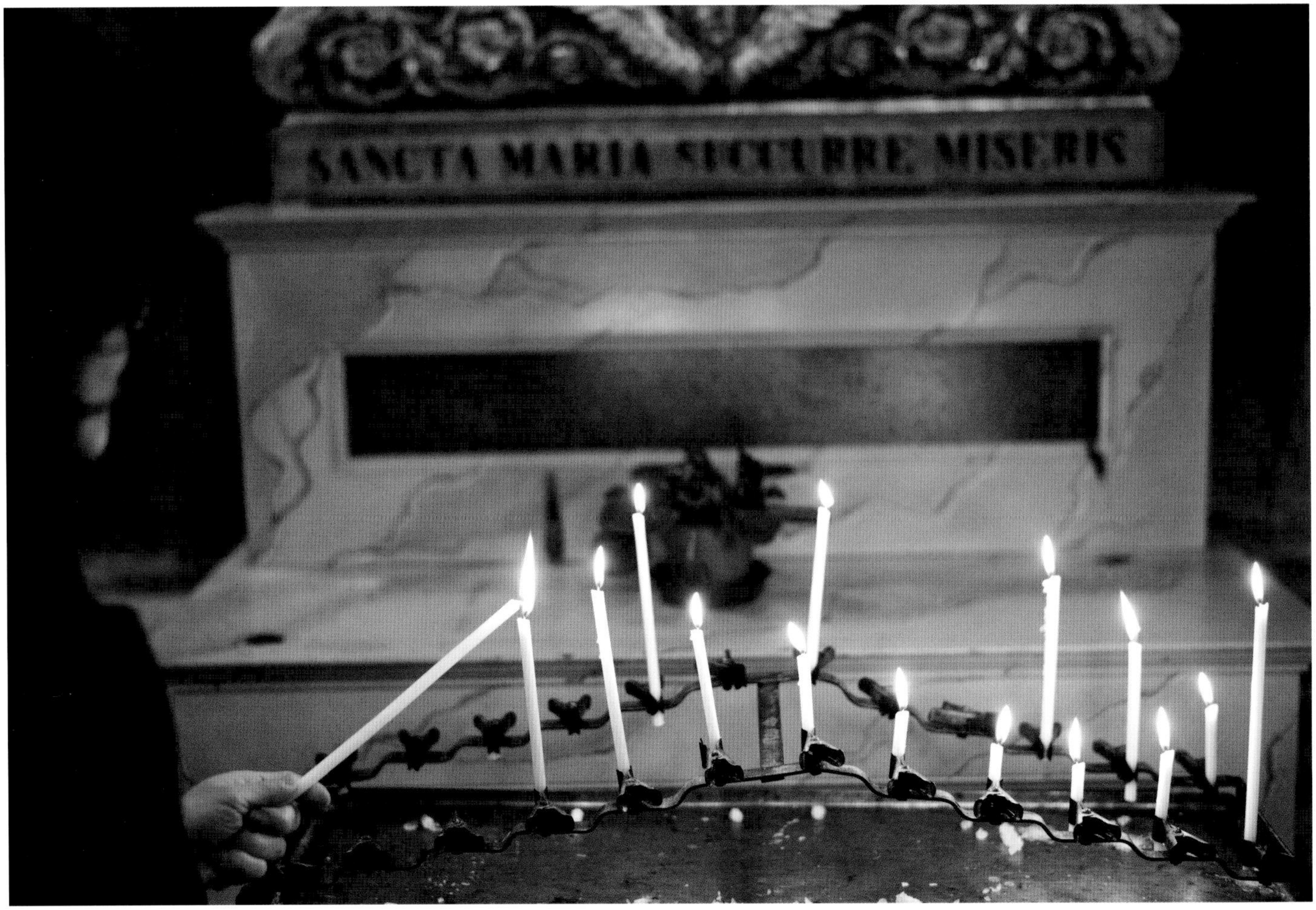
SANCTA MARIA SUCCURRE MISERIS

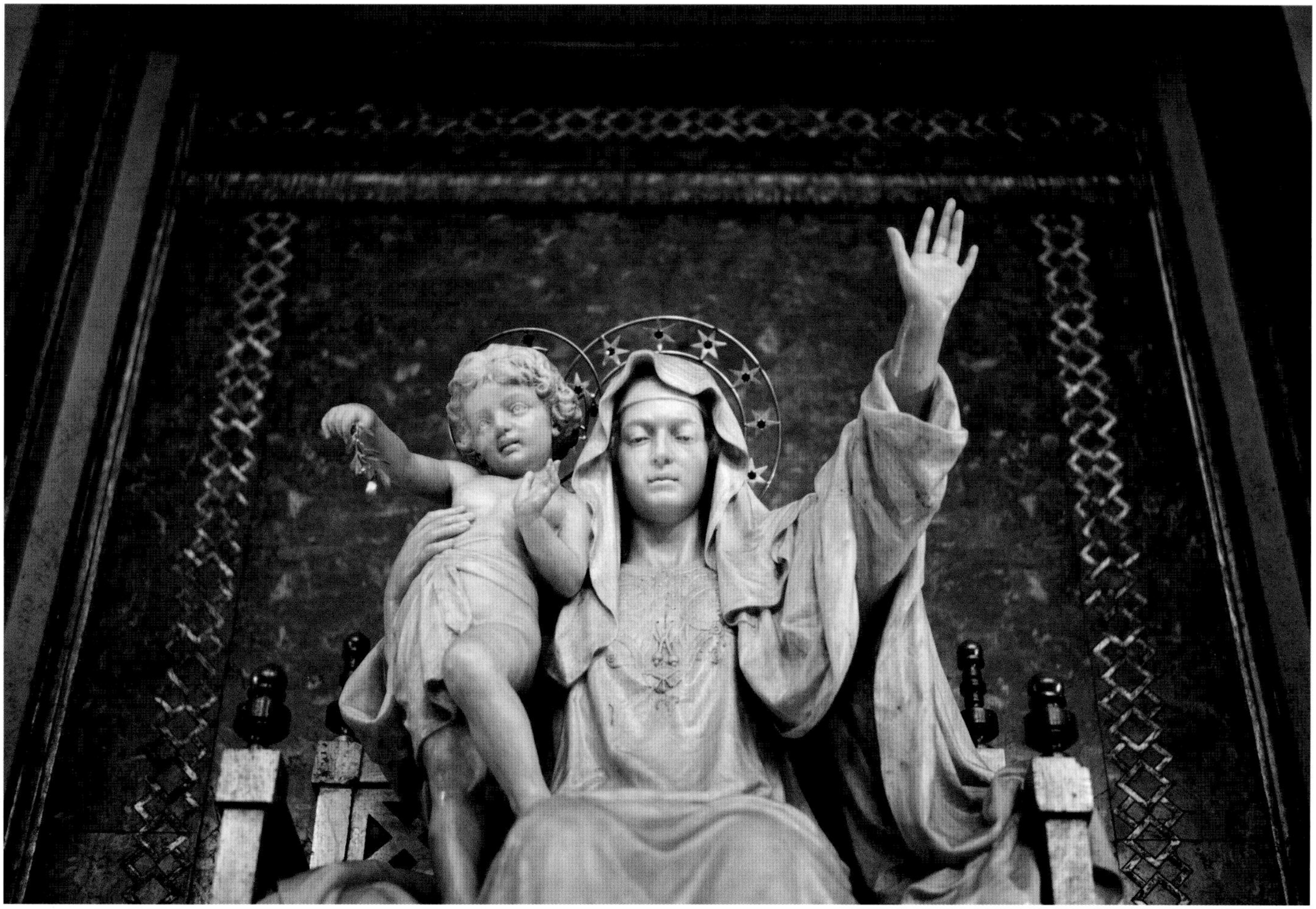

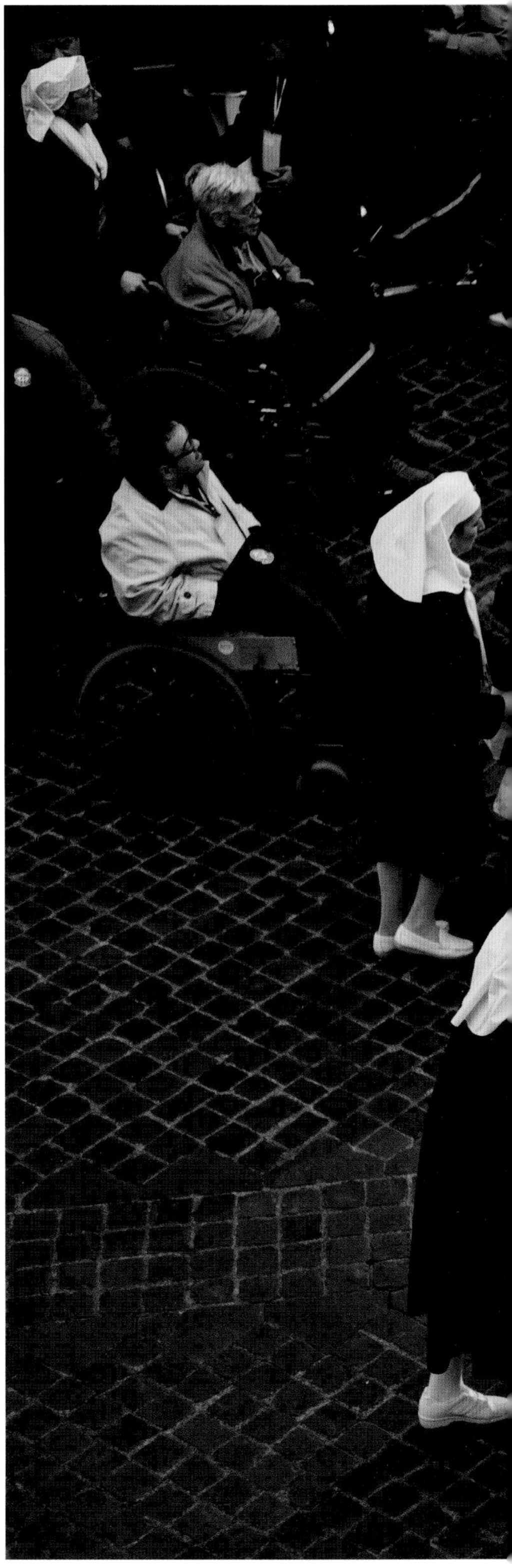

Every 8 December, the Feast of the Immaculate Conception, the Pope visits Piazza di Spagna to leave a floral tribute to the statue of Our Lady. This event is particularly popular among the Roman people. The front rows are reserved for the sick in wheelchairs. Pope Francis is especially fond of the very weakest; he offers them his time and attention, and embraces them one after the other with simple paternal affection.

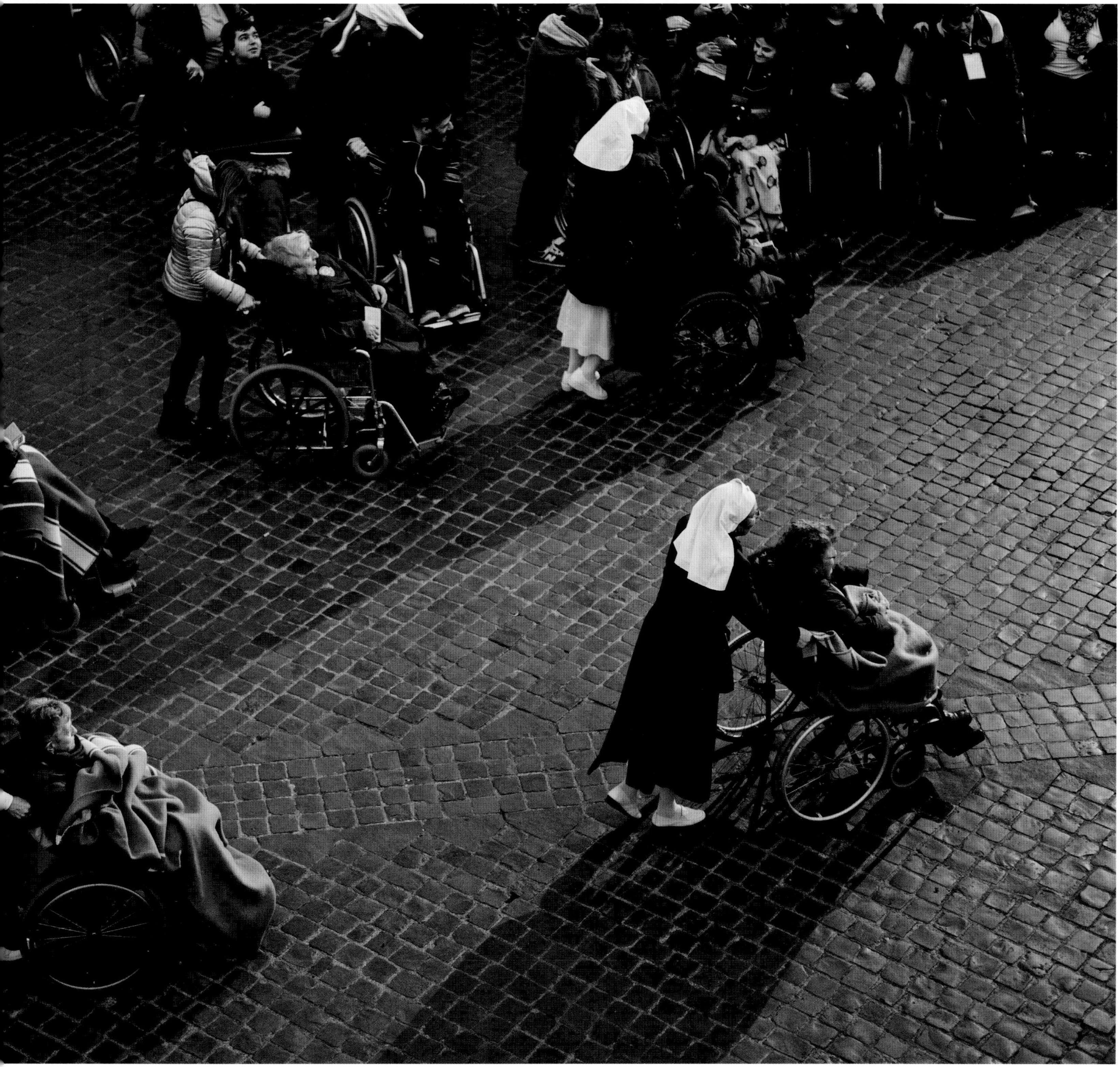

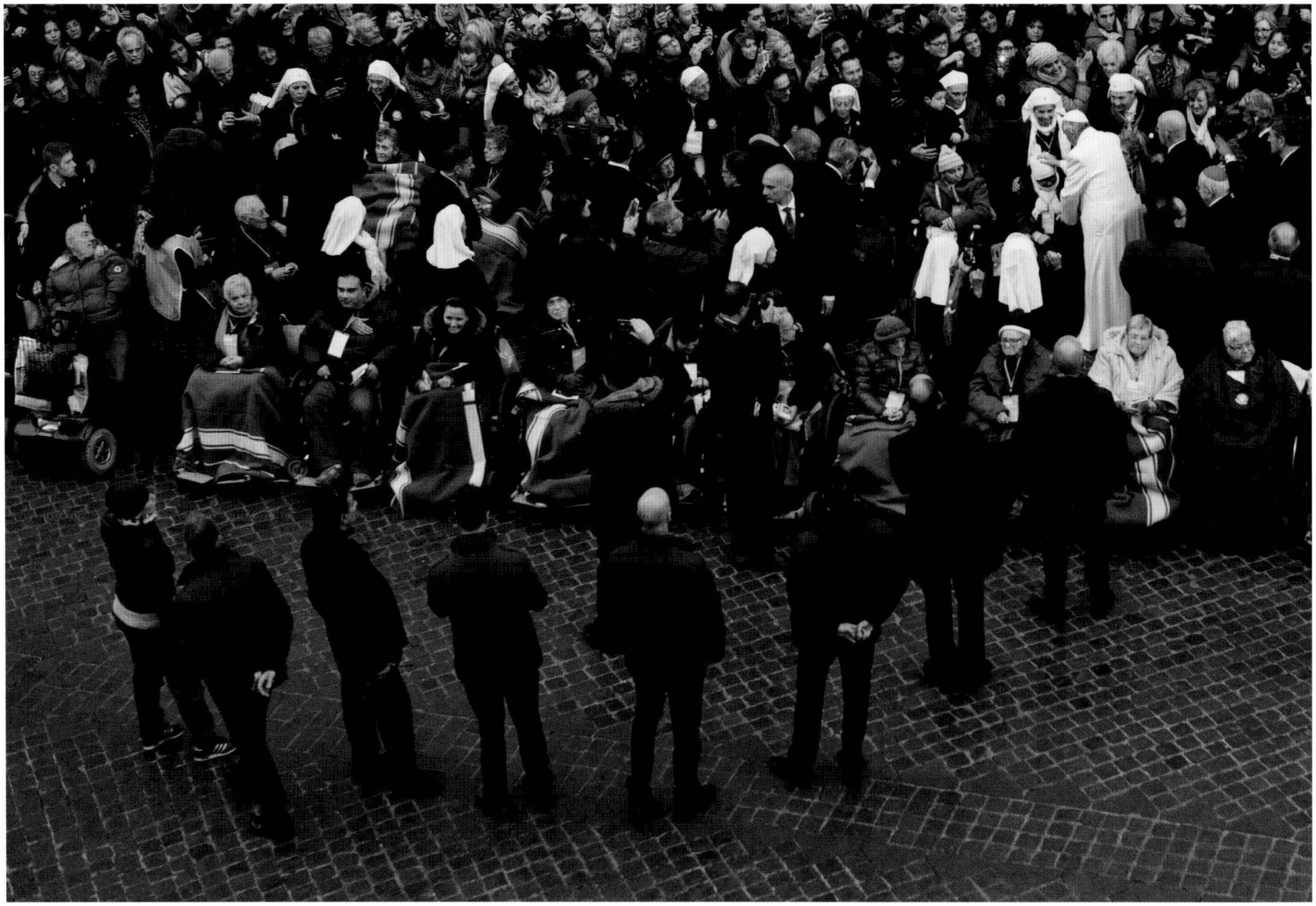

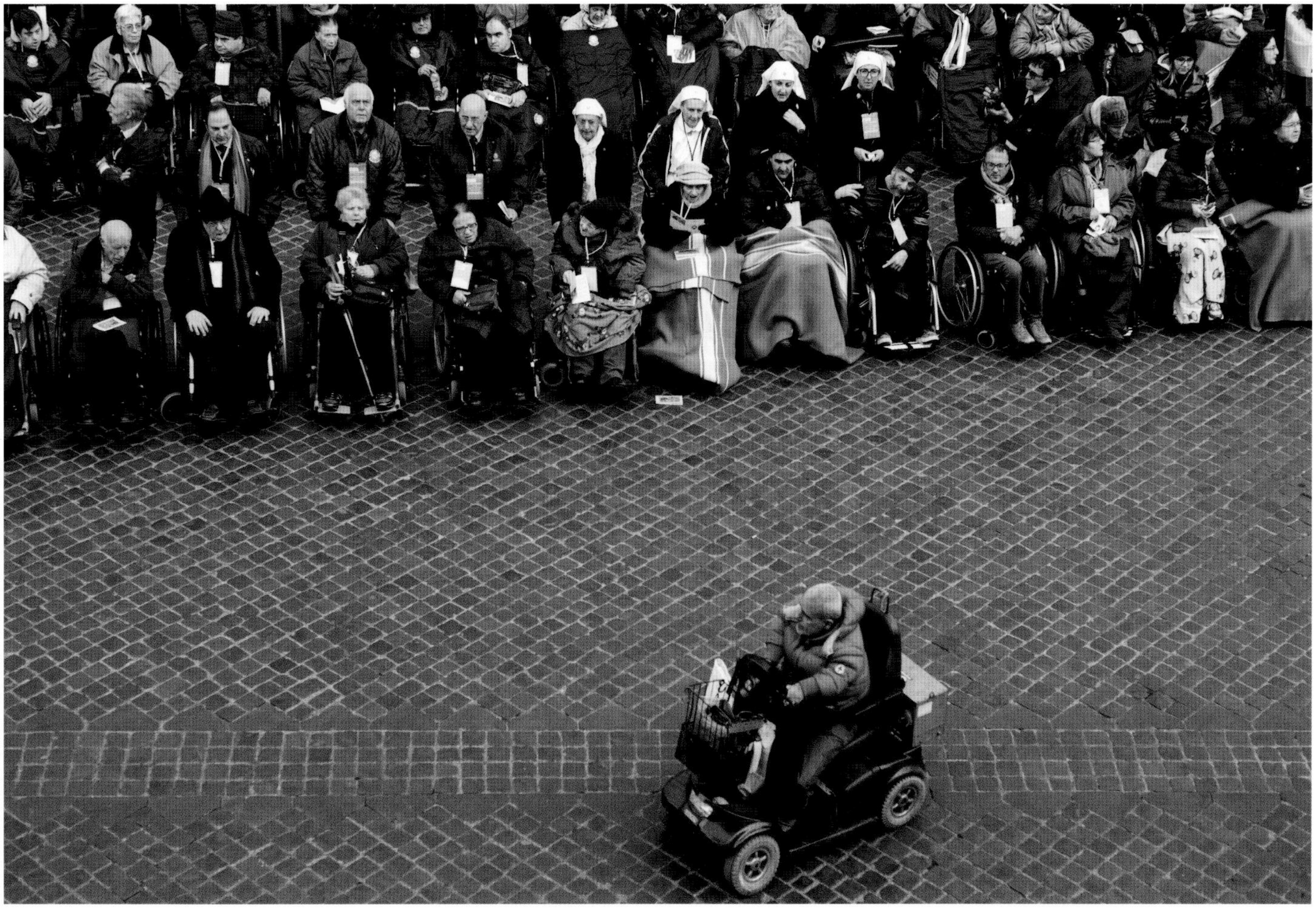

The dome of St. Peter's, designed by Michelangelo, seen from inside the Basilica. One of the largest domes ever built, it is approximately 42 metres in diameter and 130 in height, with sixteen rectangular windows that let in the light of day.

Page 36

A red rose at the feet of the tomb of Pope John Paul II. The beloved Polish pope, now a saint, was one of the great patrons of the Jubilee of Mercy. The others were Padre Pio of Pietrelcina, Mother Teresa of Calcutta, Saint Faustina Kowalska and Saint Leopold Mandić.

Page 37

The evening before the canonisation of Mother Teresa of Calcutta, the relics of the most famous nun in the world were displayed for veneration by the faithful in the Basilica of Sant'Andrea della Valle. John Paul II and Mother Teresa were friends during their lifetimes and today both are saints. It was John Paul II who beatified Mother Teresa on 19 October 2003.

On 4 September 2016, Pope Francis officially declared Mother Teresa of Calcutta a saint in the presence of thirteen heads of states and 100,000 pilgrims who had travelled to Rome from all over the world. Mother Teresa, born in Albania in 1910, founded the Missionaries of Charity in India. Her work was also honoured with the Nobel Peace Prize in 1979.

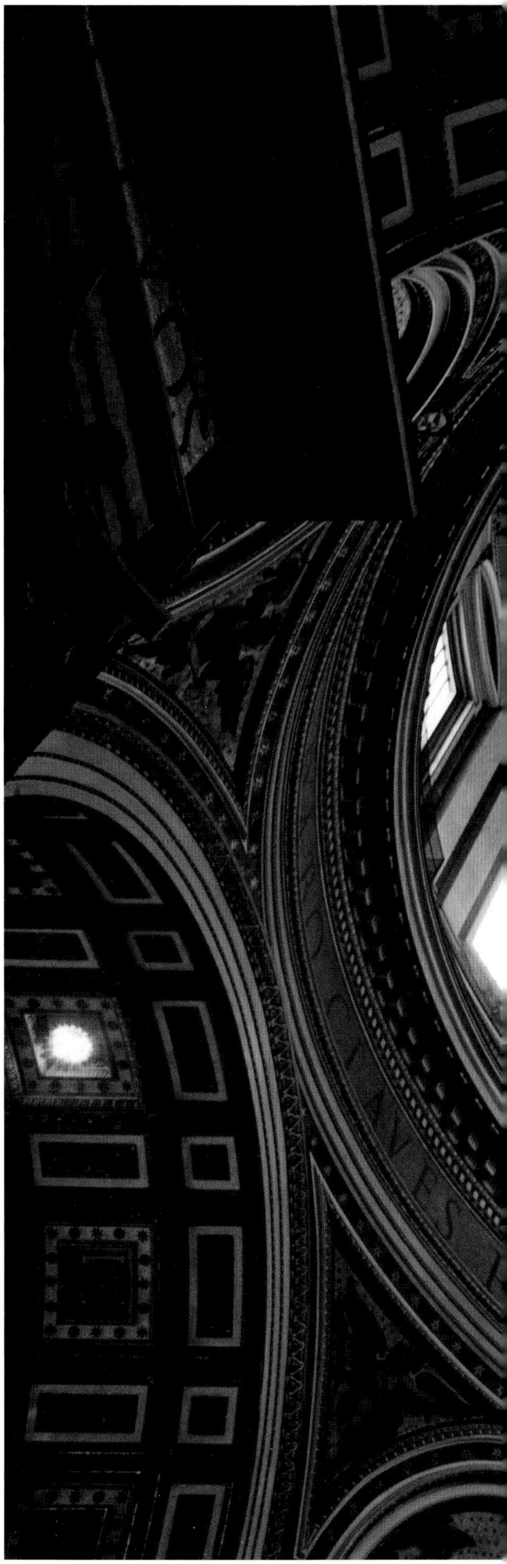

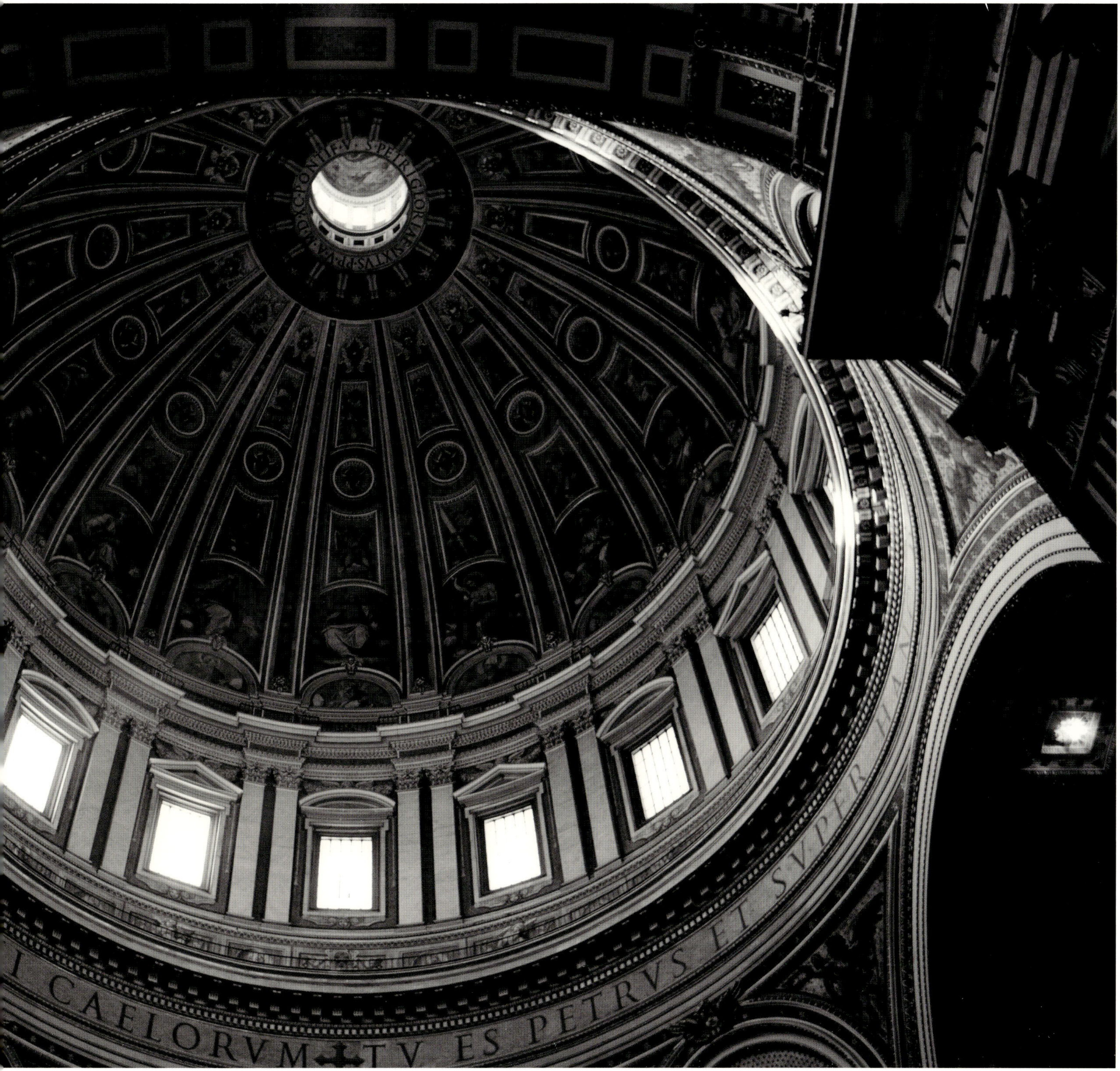
CAELORVM TV ES PETRVS ET SVPER

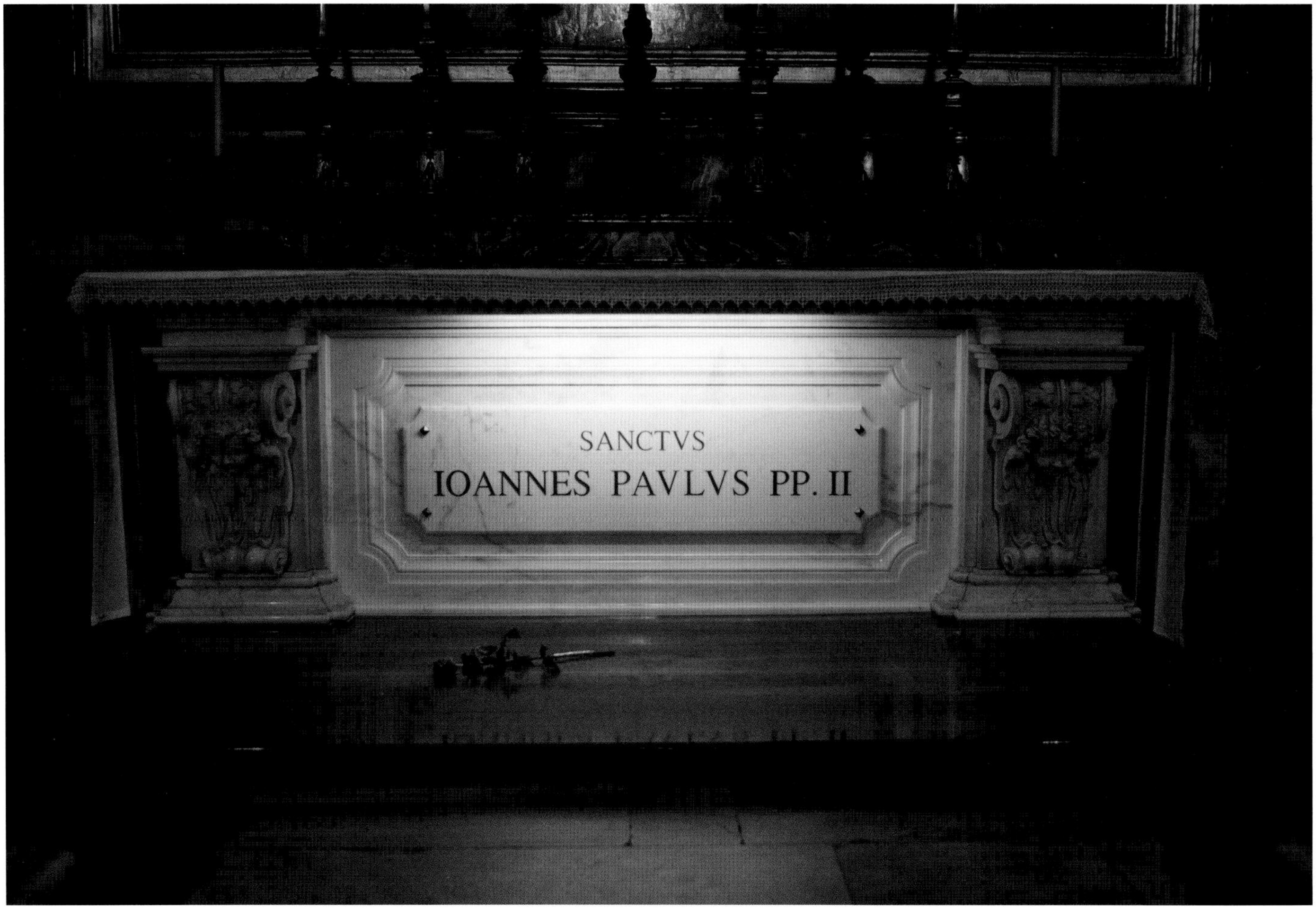
SANCTVS
IOANNES PAVLVS PP. II

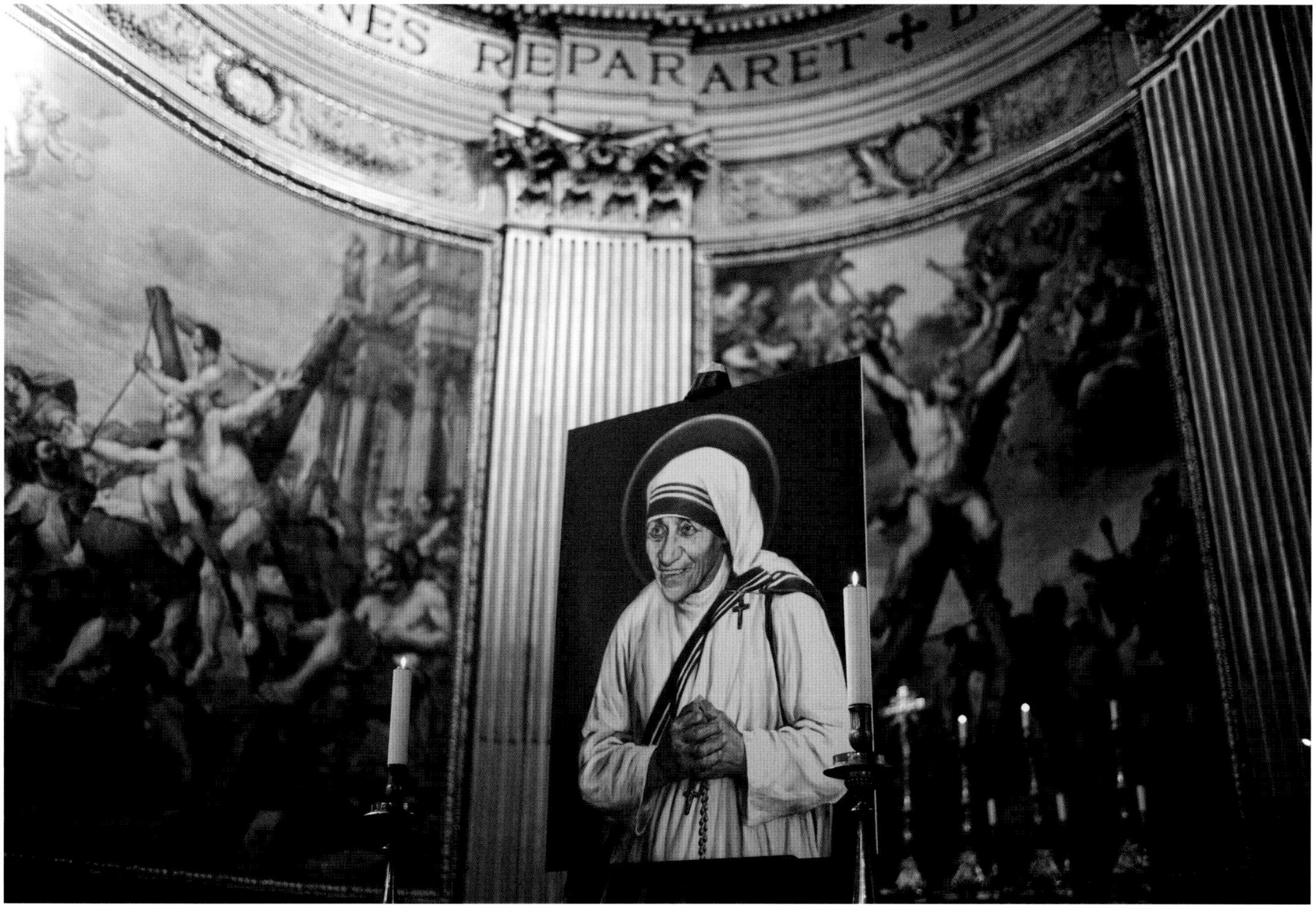
REPARARET

The priests celebrating in St. Peter's Basilica must pass before the artwork known as "the lie" by Pomarancio. The painting depicts an elderly couple who decided to sell a field to show their devotion to the apostles; they donate part of the final sum but say they have donated it all. Their lie was discovered and they were punished by death.

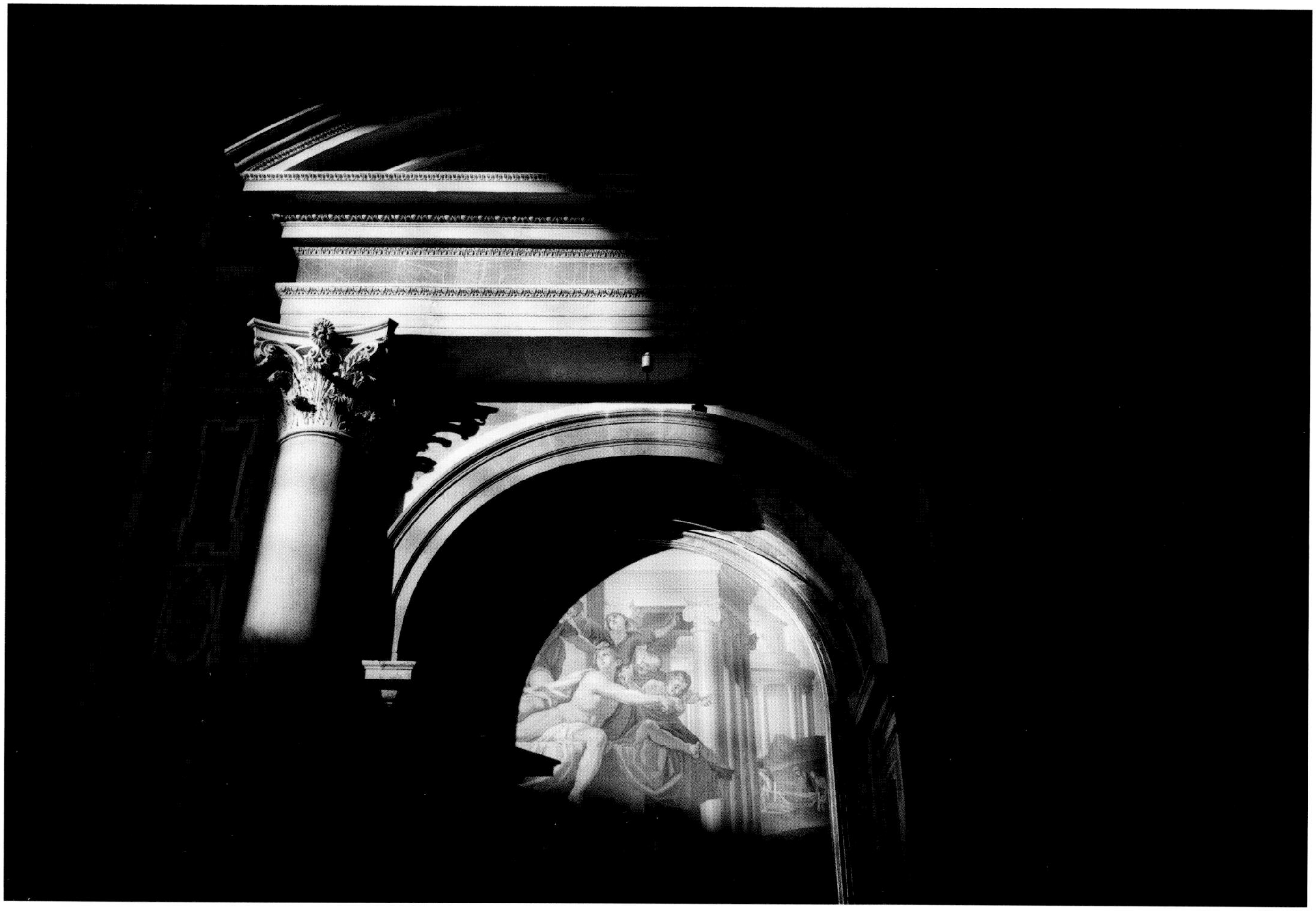

Confession is the sacrament of forgiveness. Through the absolution of sins by the priest, God offers his pardon and peace to the repentant believer.

Padre Pio of Pietrelcina spent hours in the confessional. He was considered a great confessor; many said that the monk could see into their souls and would sometimes list the sins of the penitent kneeling before him without leaving any room for ambiguity.

Pages 42-45

The streets of Rome are invaded by processions organised by various religious orders and the parishes for the Feast of the Immaculate Conception. Some traditional young seminarists sing "Praise to Our Lady" while the pilgrims are gathered in prayer with lit candles.

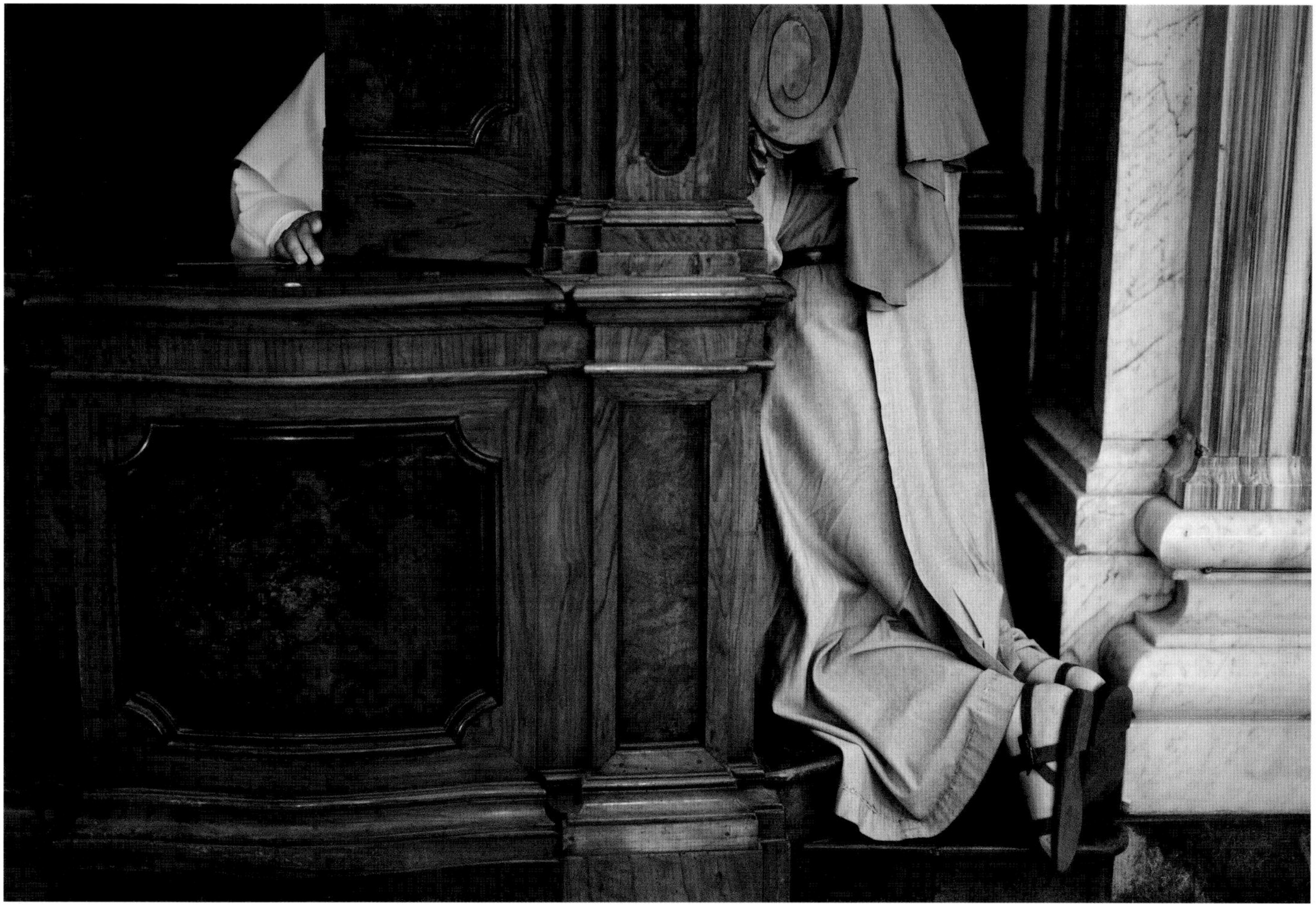

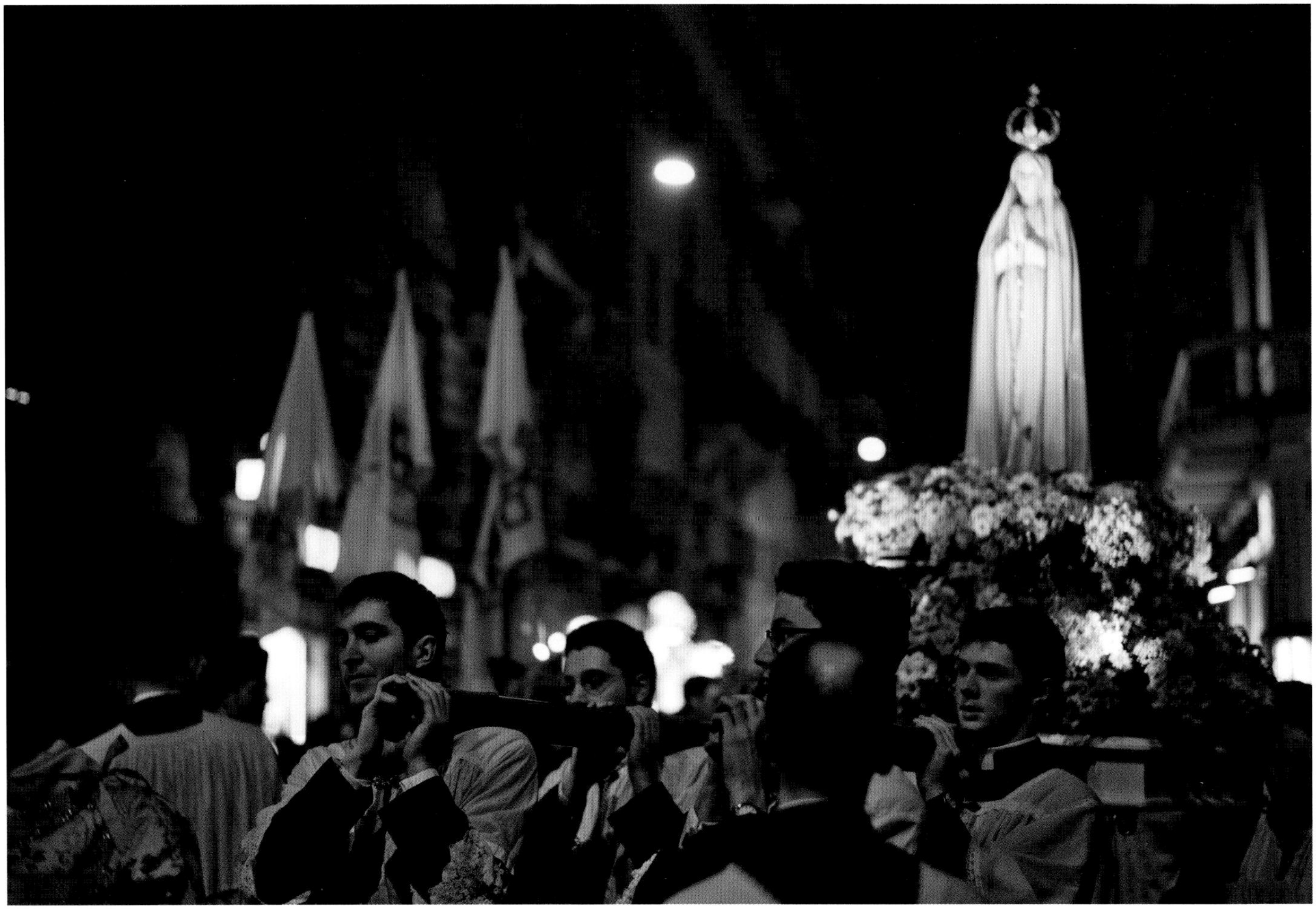

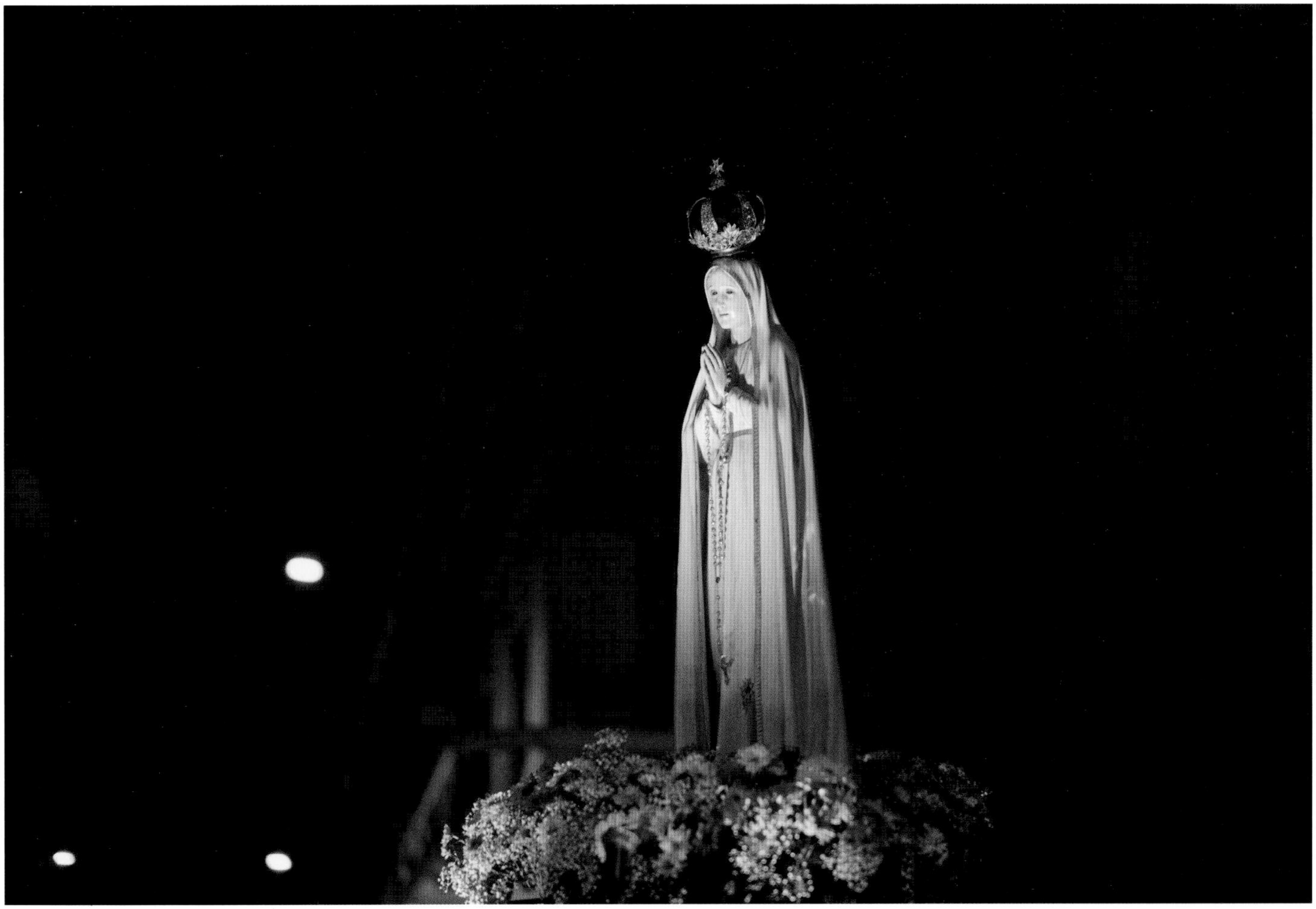

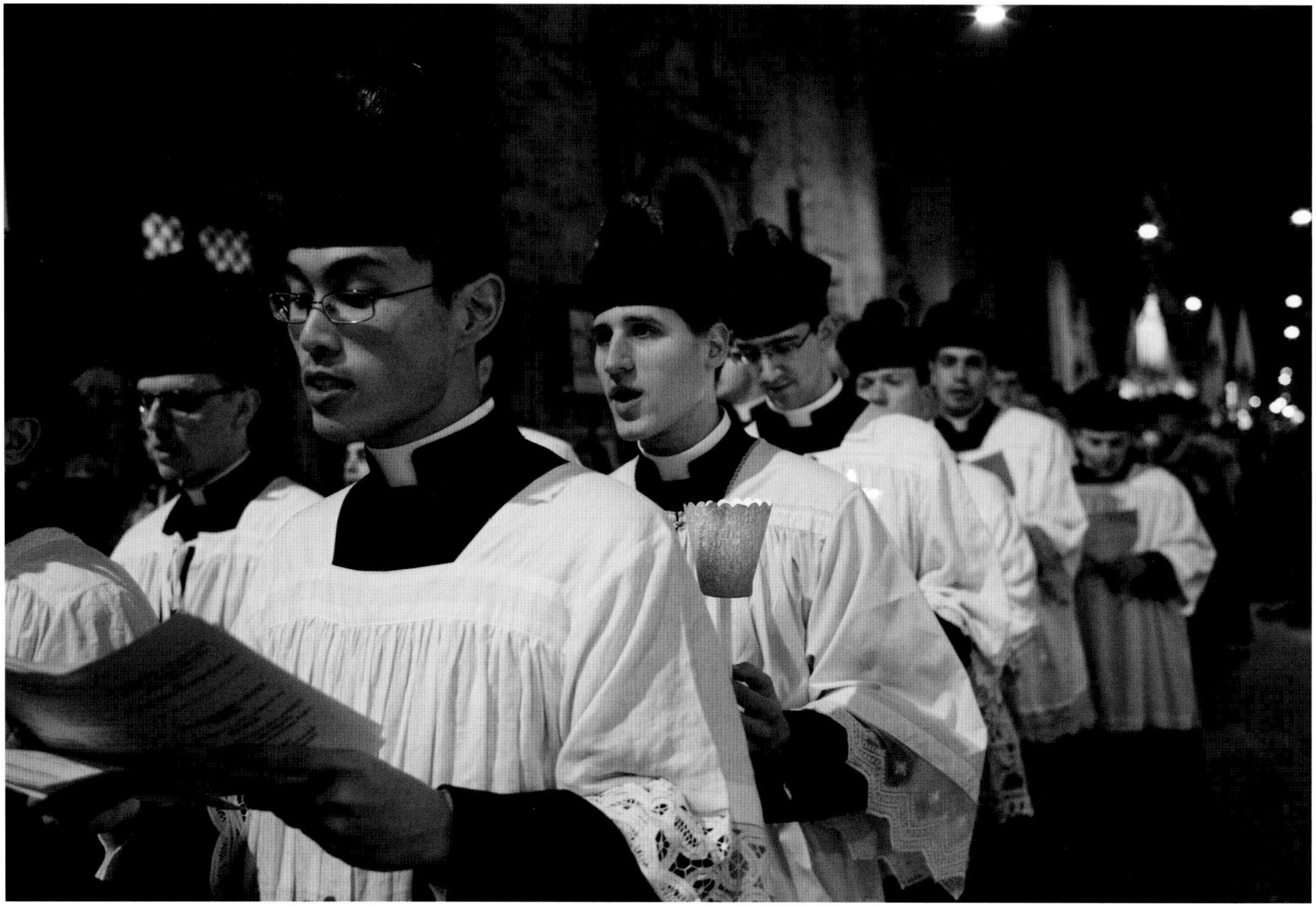

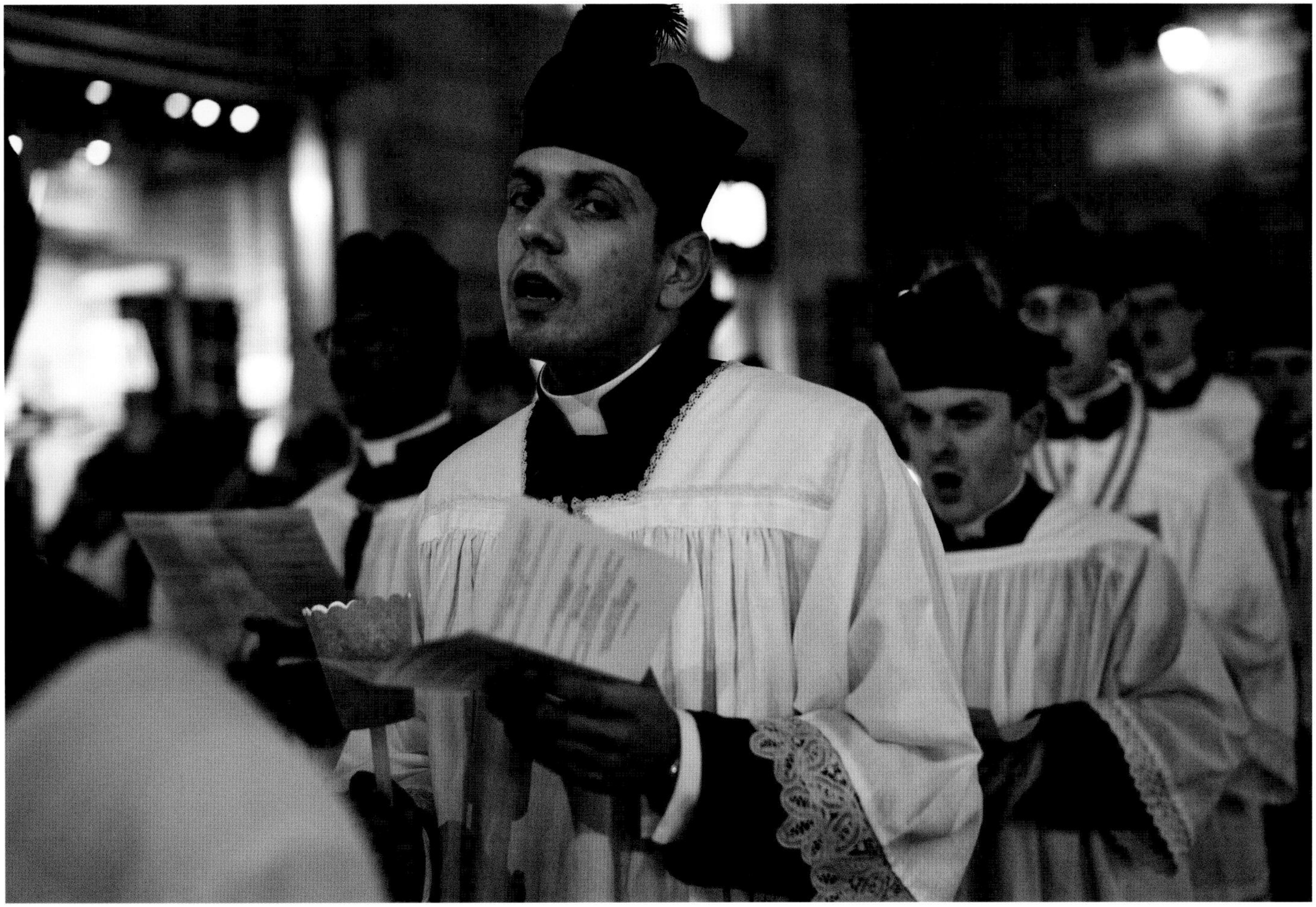

The rosary is a beaded necklace that guides meditation on the mysteries or important events in the lives of Jesus and his mother Mary. This devotion was made popular by St. Dominic. Catholic tradition states that he received the first rosary in 1214 during an apparition of Our Lady.

Pages 48-49

A large number of armed forces were deployed to provide security during the Jubilee year in Rome. Approximately 2 300 soldiers guarded the sensitive sites and parts of the Vatican, where 200 new cameras were also installed. All pilgrims, including cardinals, bishops and nuns had to pass through a metal detector and have their bags checked in order to enter the Roman basilicas. Some were also searched.

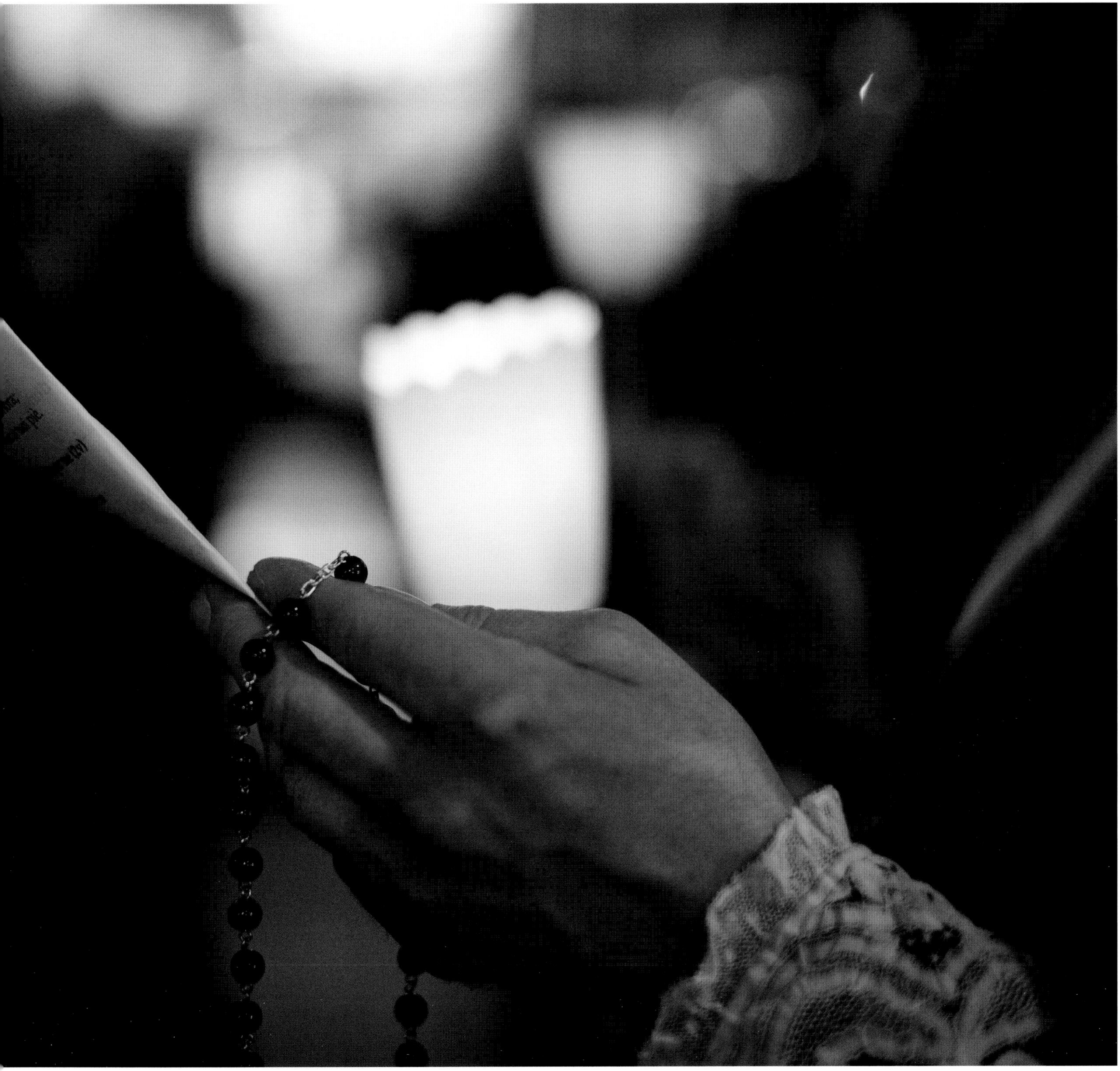

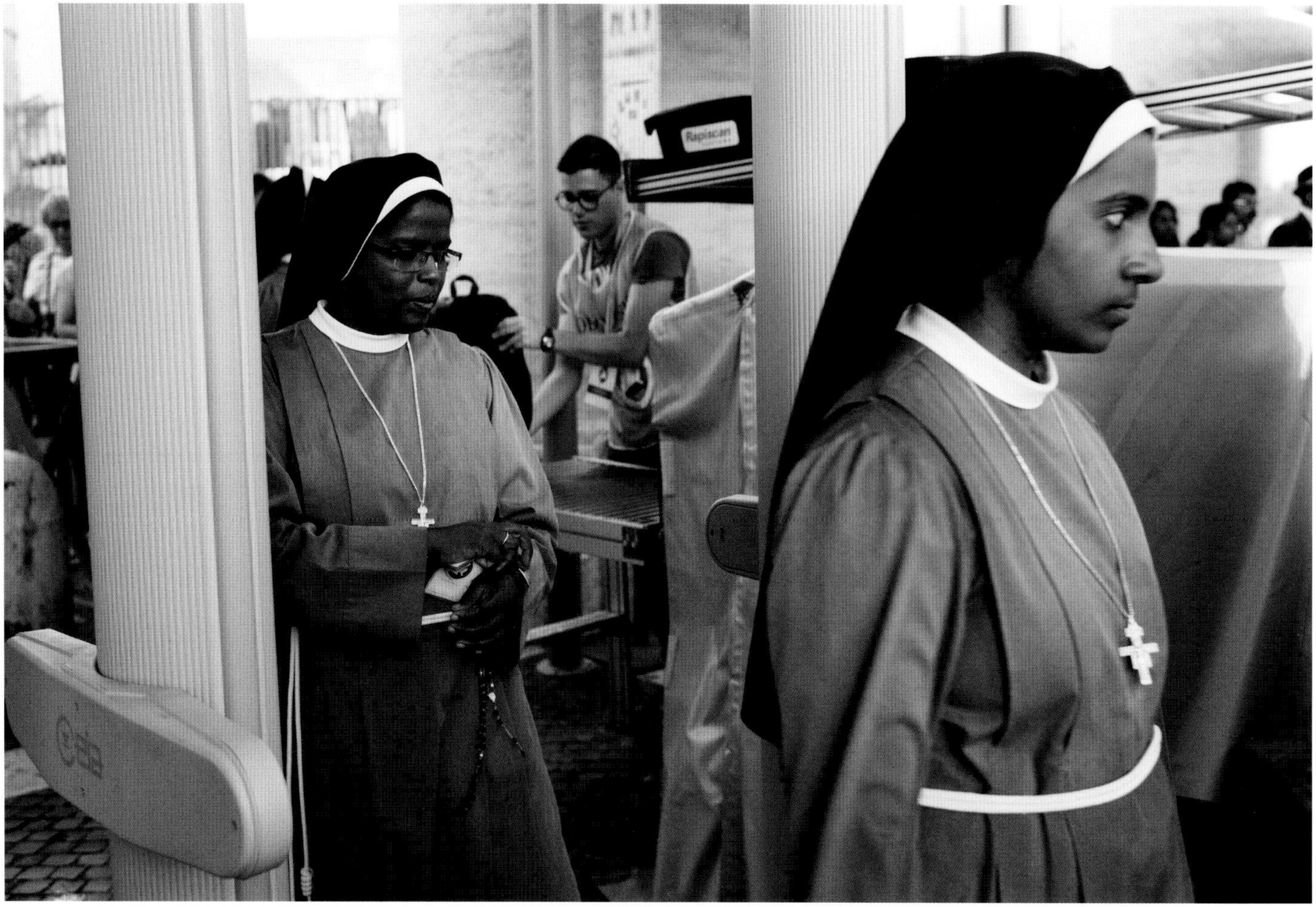
Rapiscan

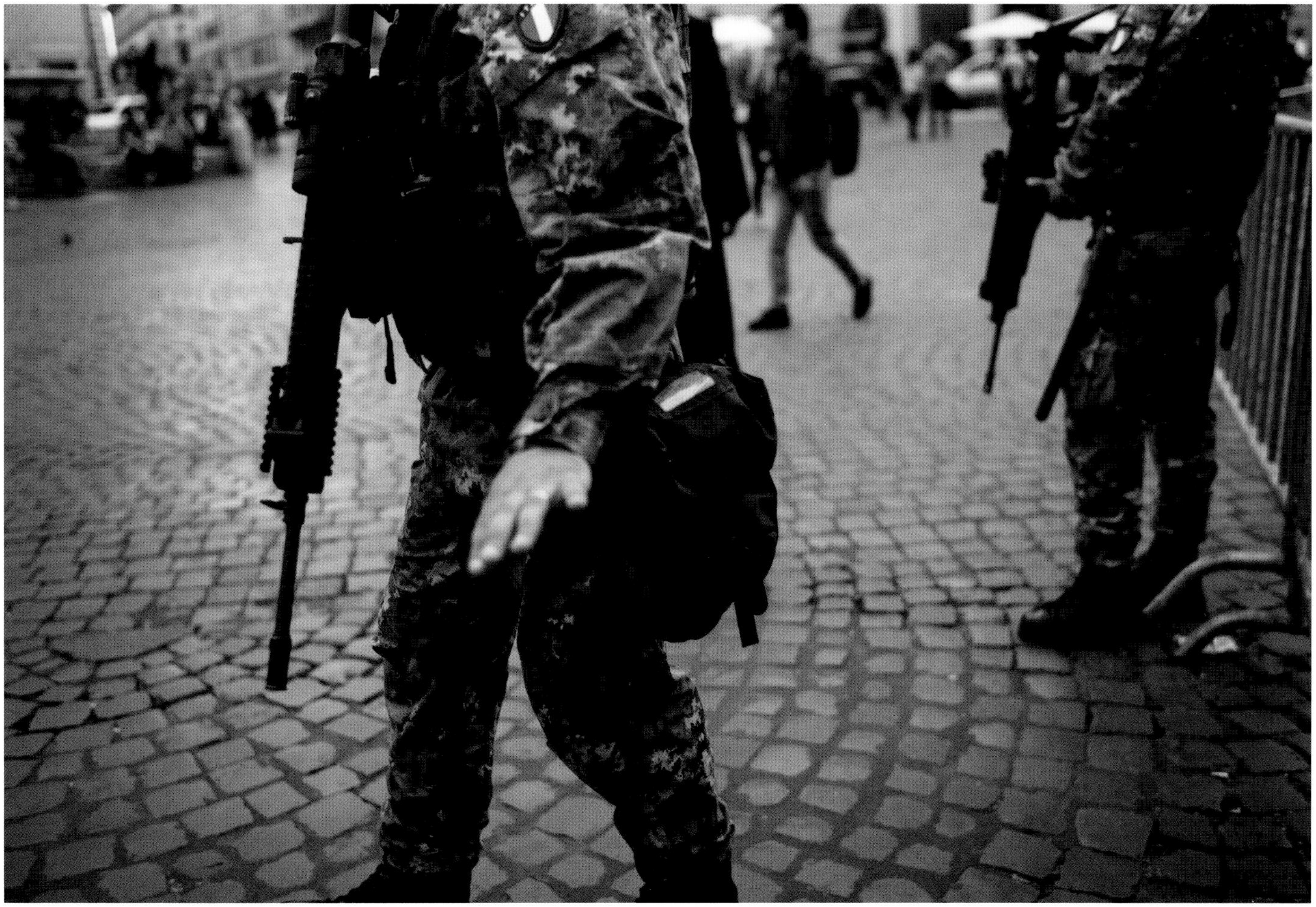

On 13 December 2015, Pope Francis opened the Holy Door of the Archbasilica of St. John Lateran. The ceremony was smaller and more intimate than the ceremony at St. Peter's as it was held inside the basilica.

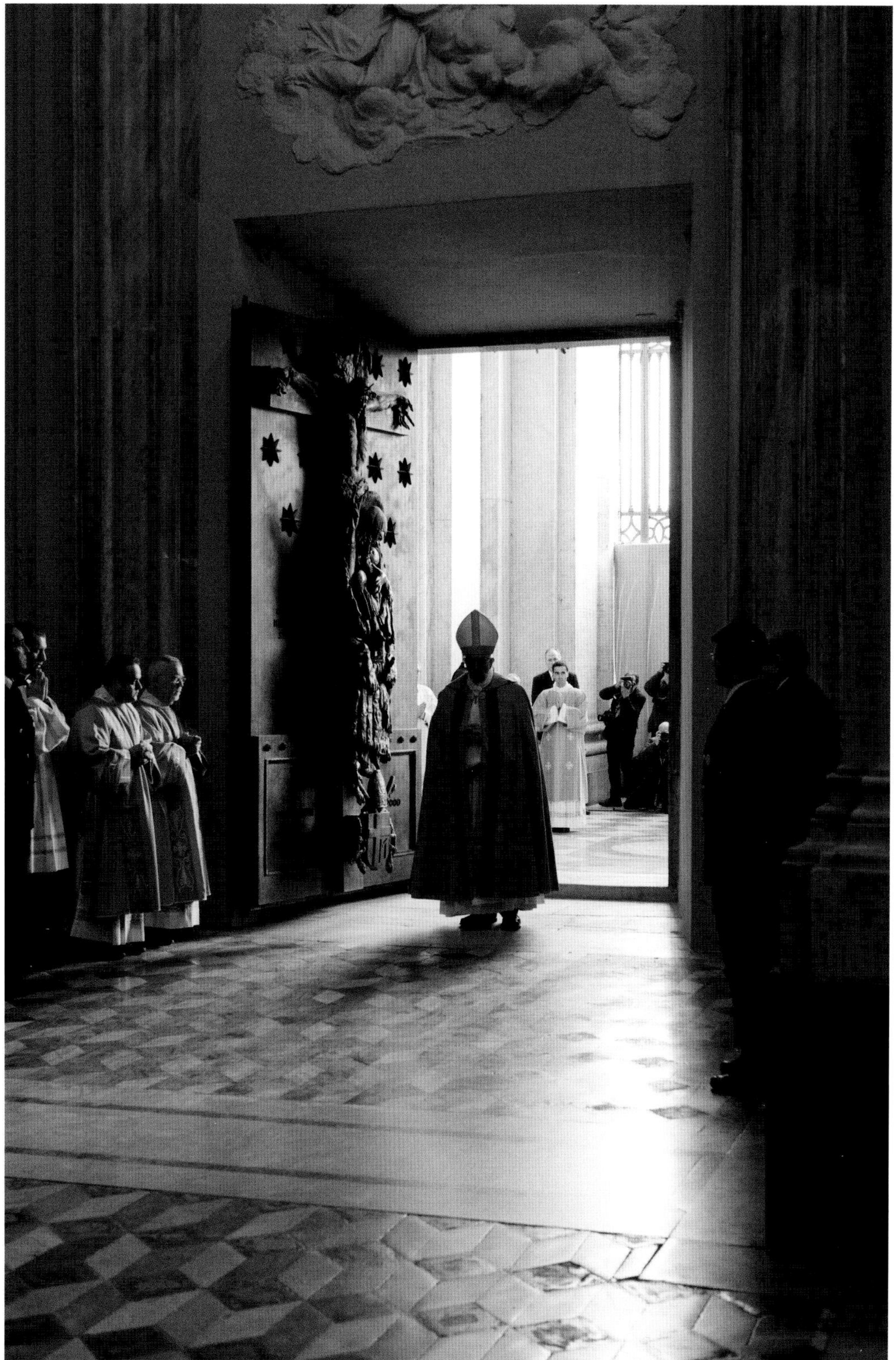

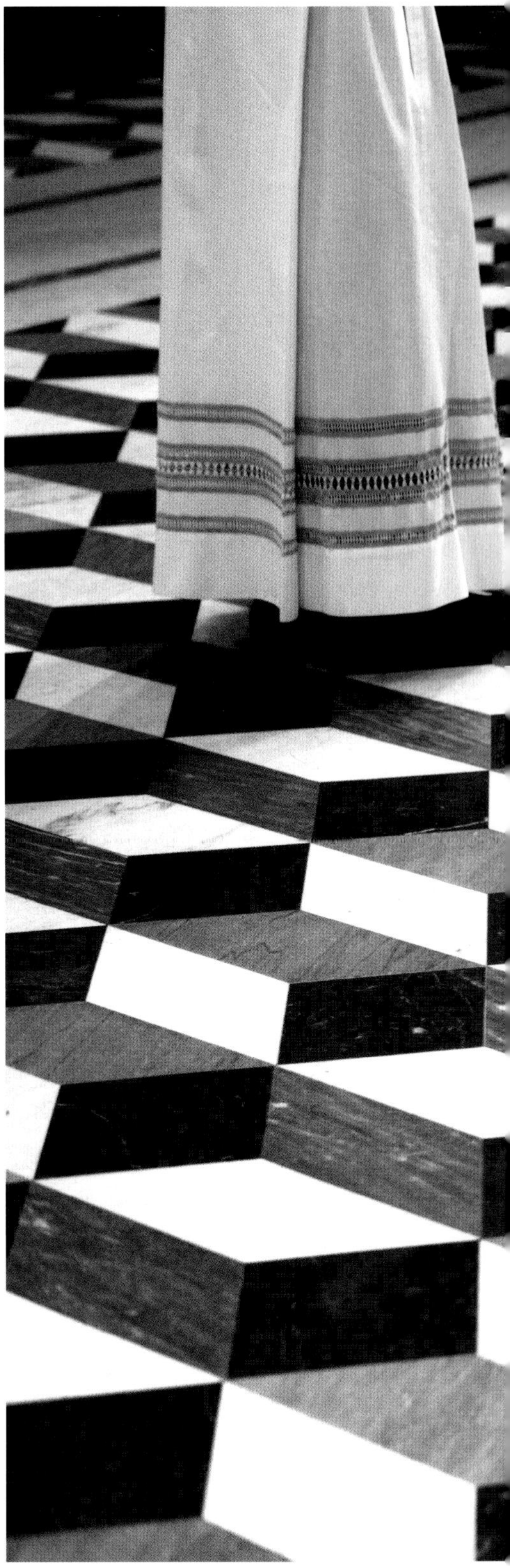

The geometric flooring of the Archbasilica of St. John Lateran captures the attention of each visitor. The Cosmatesque floor is ancient but seems so modern.

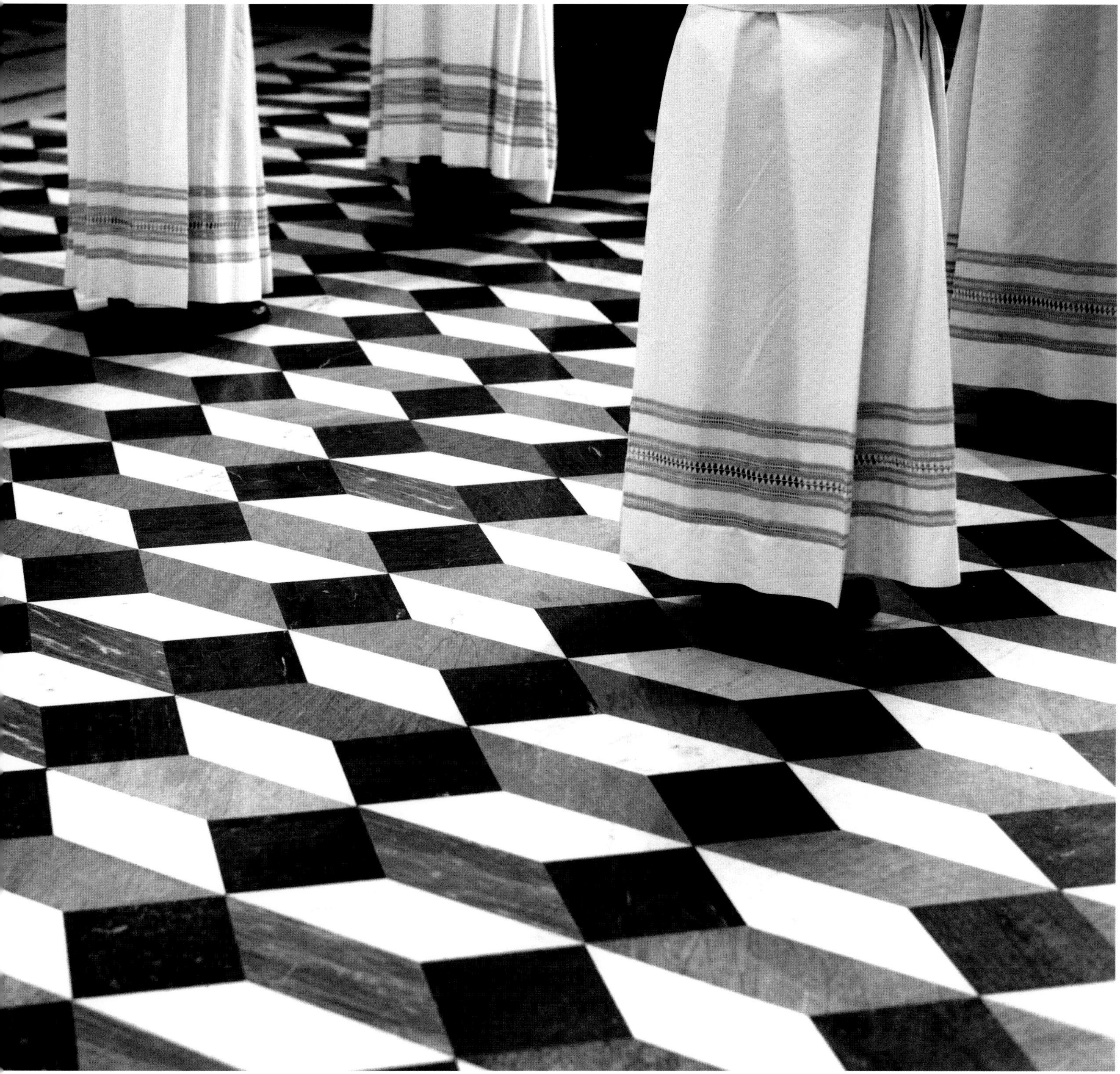

It was in the Archbasilica of St. John Lateran in 1300 that Pope Boniface VIII announced the beginning of the very first Jubilee of the Church, looking down from the Loggia delle Benedizioni.

Pages 56-57

A woman prays on her knees in one of the chapels of Santa Maria Maggiore. The composition recalls the same position skilfully depicted by Caravaggio in his 1604 painting *Madonna dei Pelligrini,* which hangs in the Church of Sant'Agostino in Rome. Though 400 years have passed, the gestures and symbols remain the same.

Pages 58-59

The gold crosses and rings of the bishops contrast with the wooden crosses and bare hands of the nuns. Pope Francis has often criticised the luxurious lives of the cardinals and bishops as well as the corruption and financial scandal within the Holy See.

Pages 60-61

Every Wednesday throughout the Jubilee year, the Pope dedicated his general audience to exploring the theme of mercy. The general audience is a moment for public reflection when the faithful can meet the pontiff. Pope Francis loves spending time greeting the faithful and pays particular attention to the elderly and disabled.

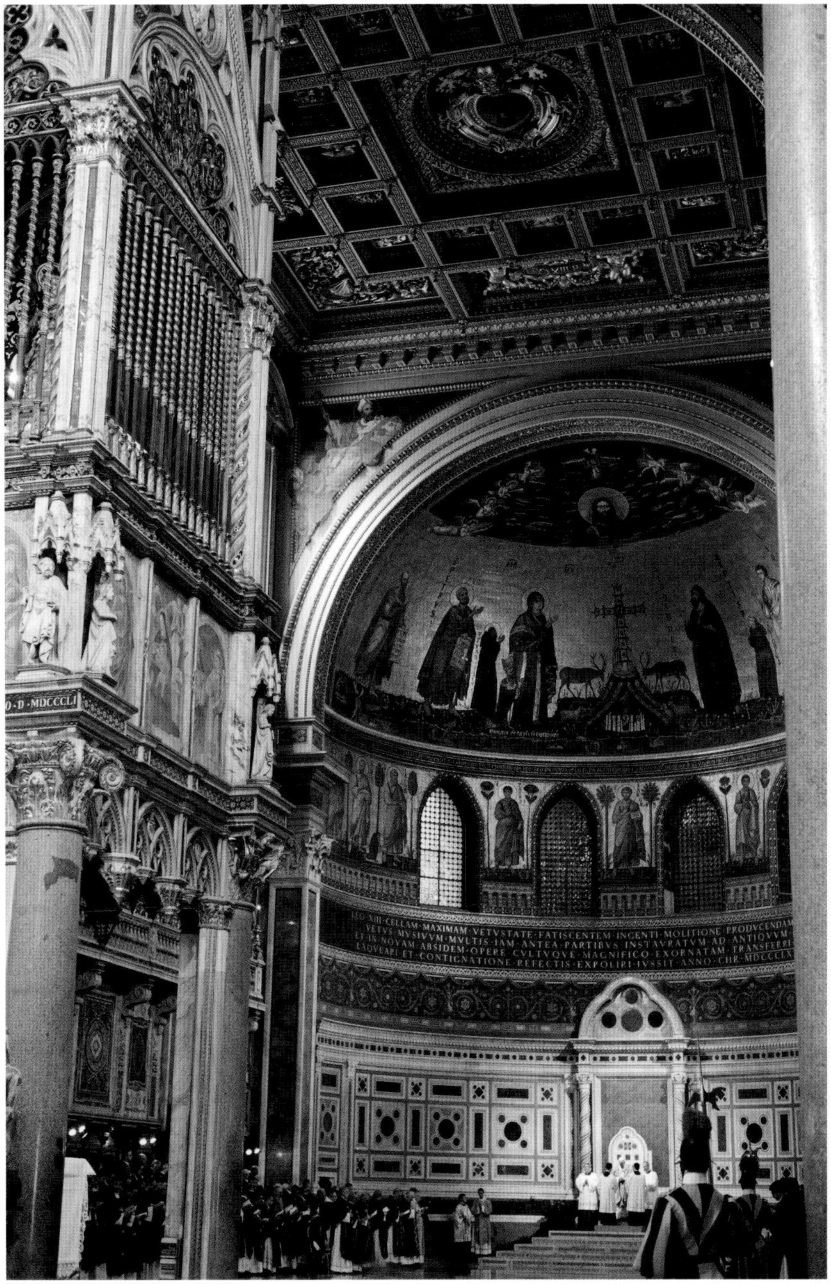
LEO XIII CELLAM MAXIMAM VETVSTATE FATISCENTEM INGENTI MOLITIONE PRODVCENDAM
VETVS MVSIVVM MVLTIS IAM ANTEA PARTIBVS INSTAVRATVM AD ANTIQVVM
ET IN NOVAM ABSIDEM OPERE CVLTVQVE MAGNIFICO EXORNATAM TRANSFERRI
LAQVEARI ET CONTIGNATIONE REFECTIS EXPOLIRI IVSSIT ANNO CHR MDCCCLX

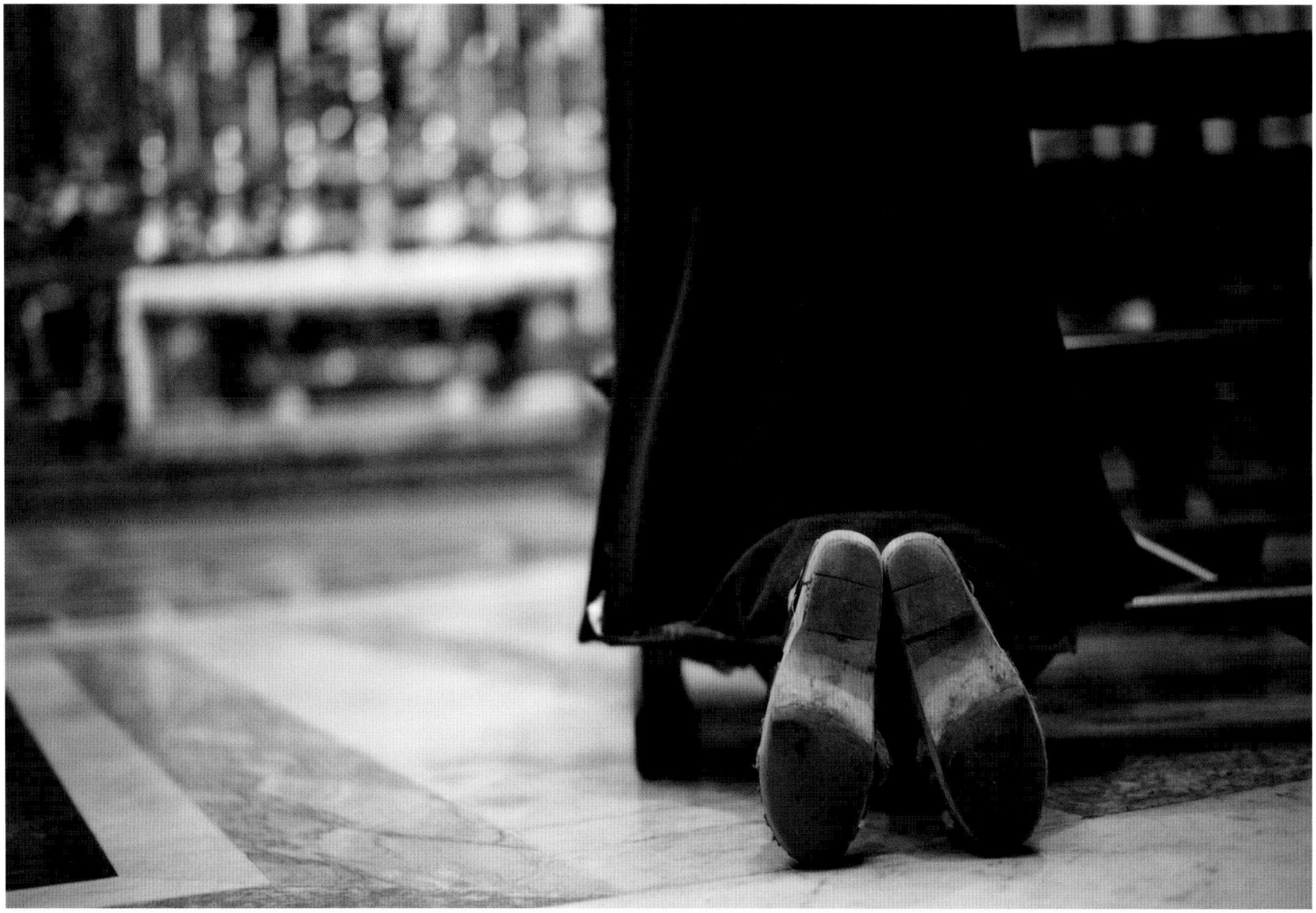

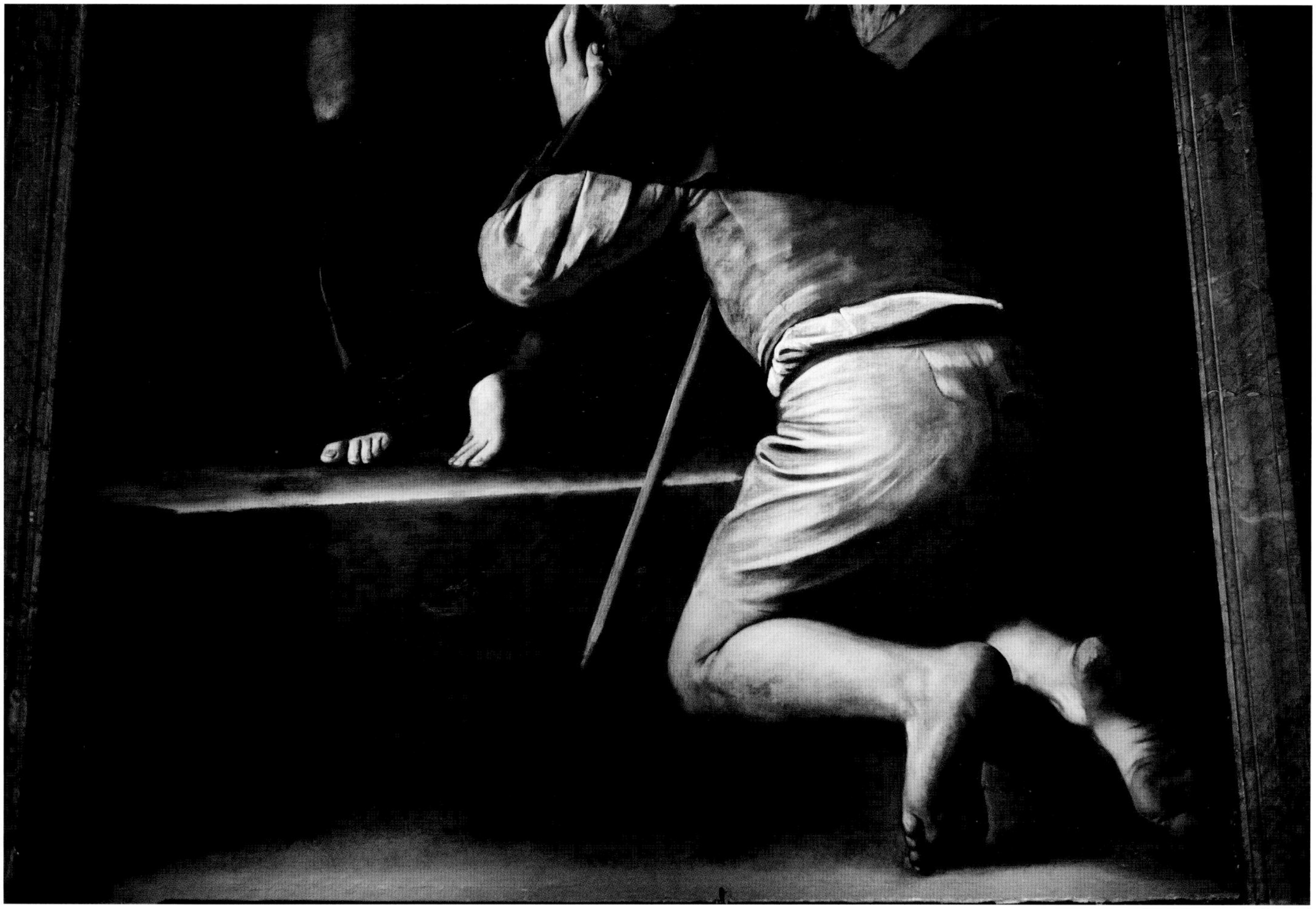

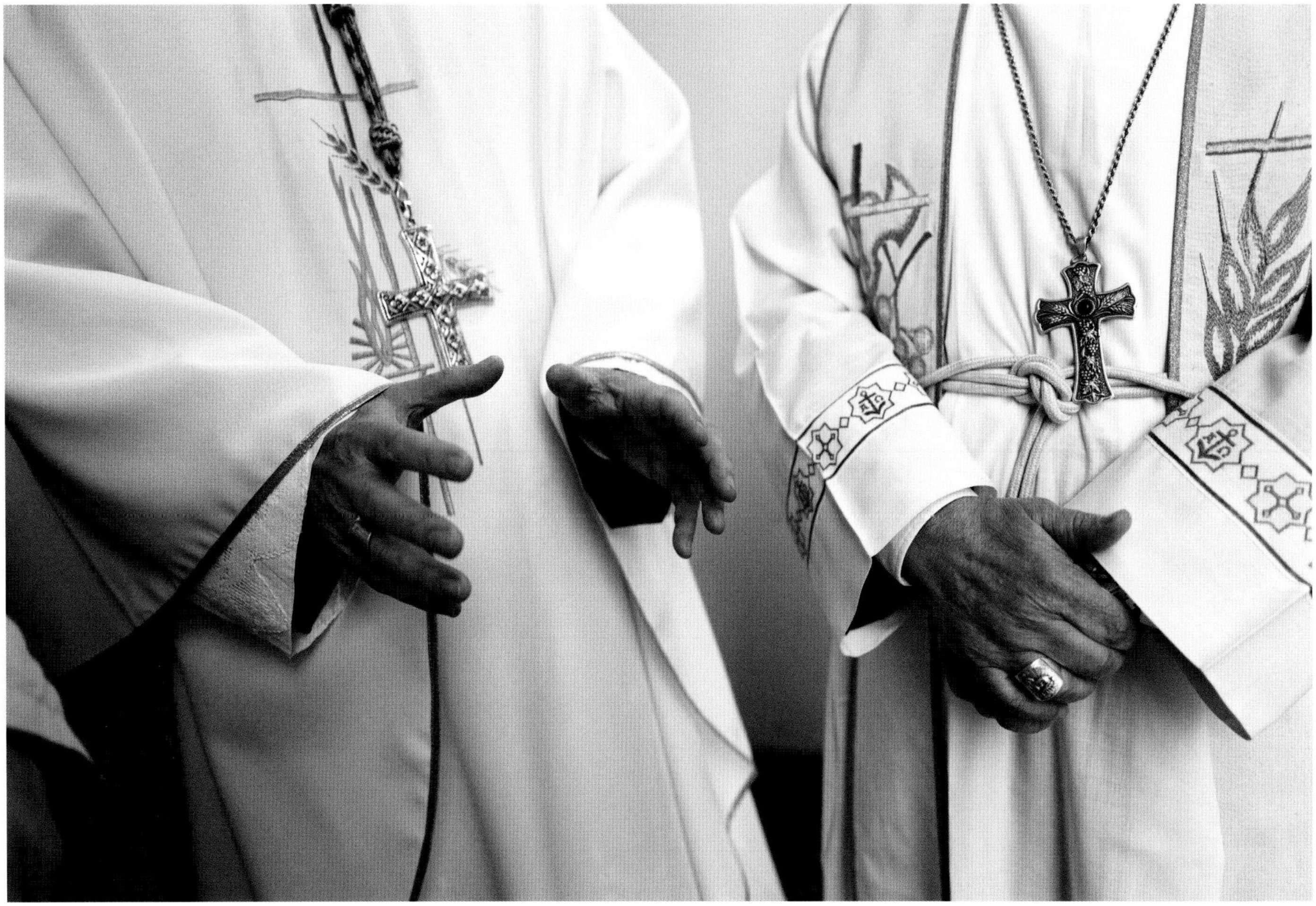

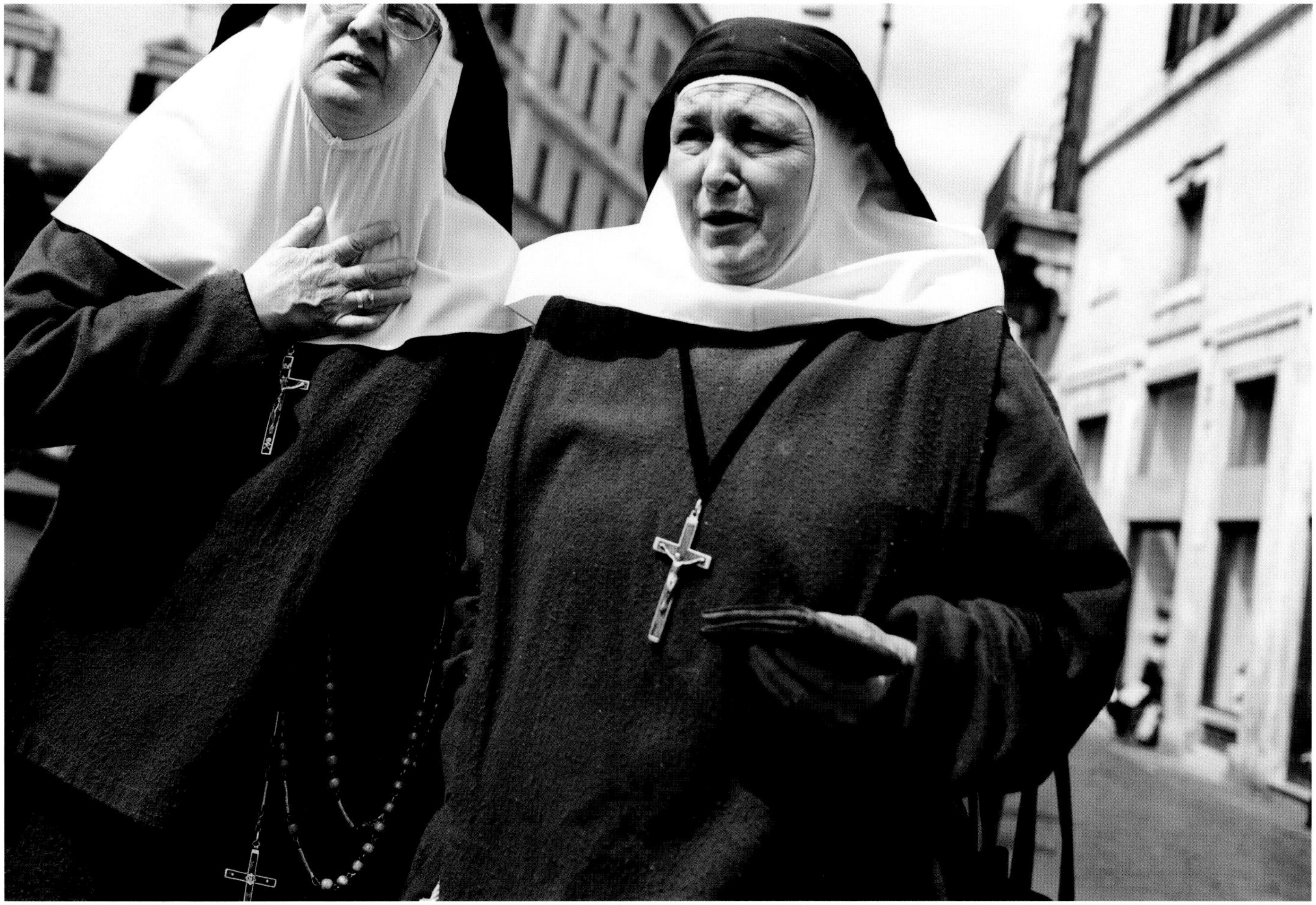

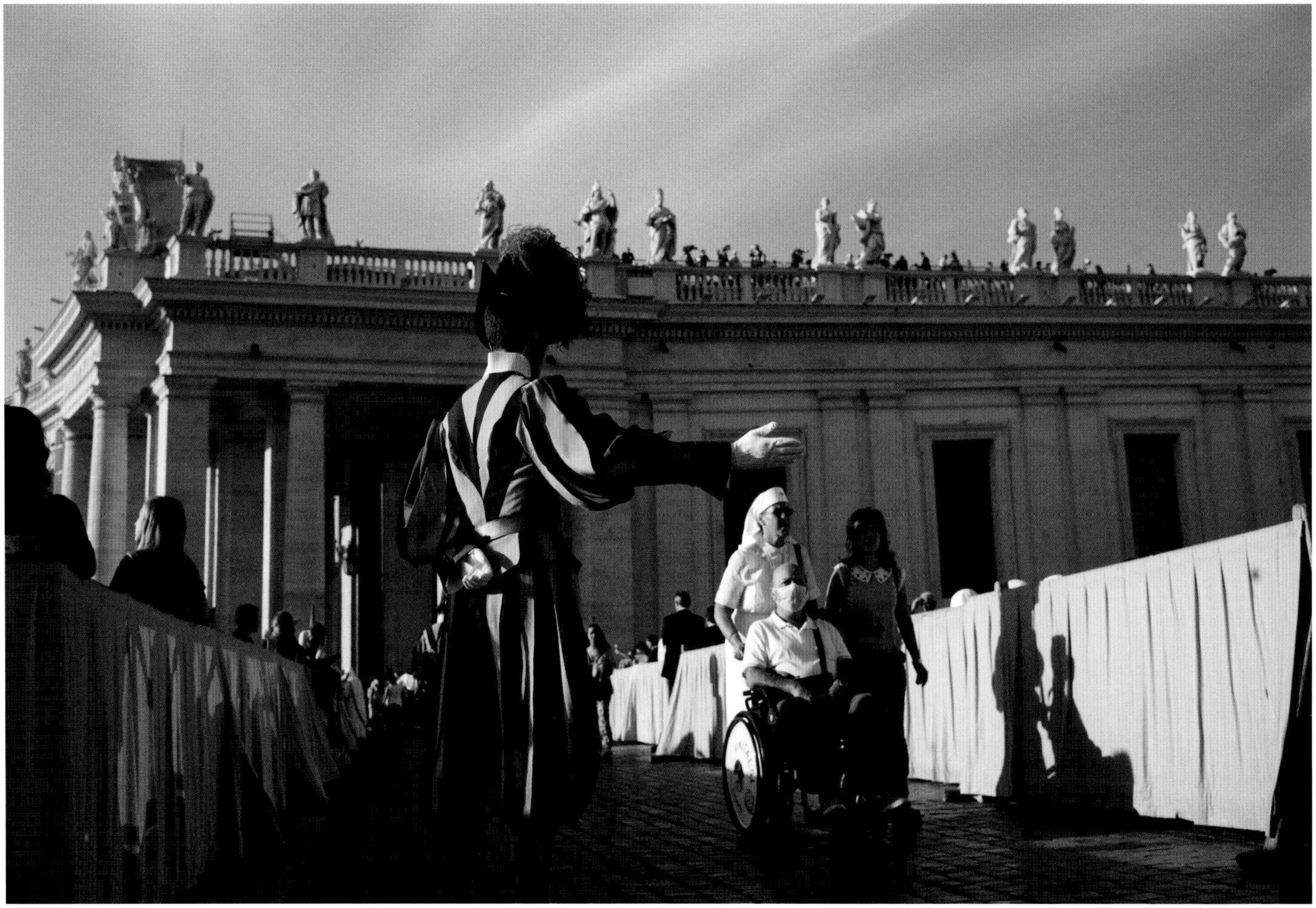

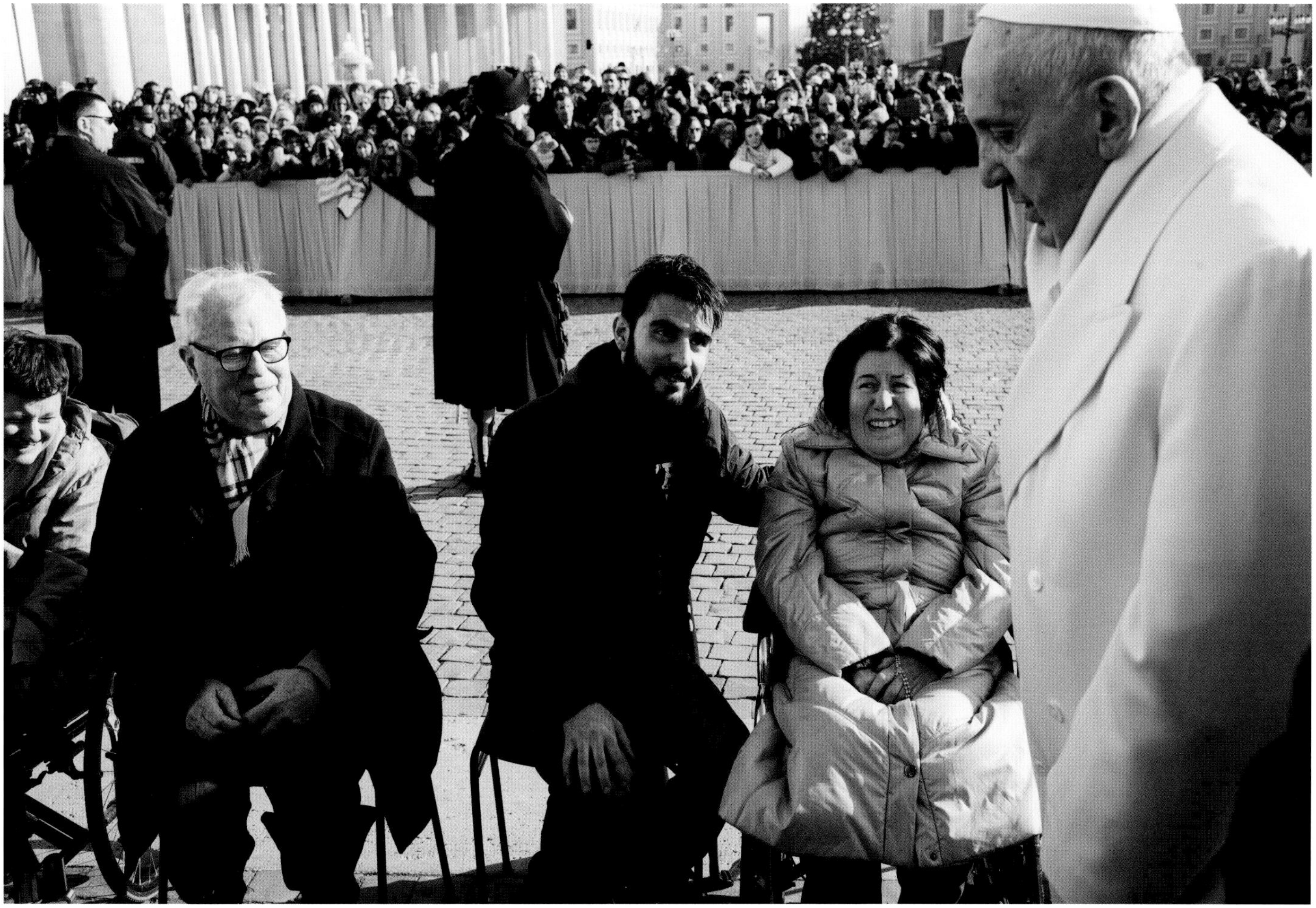

Behind this door begins the life of hundreds of detainees in Regina Coeli, the most known prison in Rome, also because it is located in the central district of Trastevere. Four popes of modern times travelled from the Vatican to visit Regina Coeli: John XXIII in 1958, Paul VI in 1964, John Paul II in 2000 and Benedict XVI in 2011. Built as a convent in 1654, since 1881 it has housed the prison bearing the name of Mary, mother of god, Regina Coeli.

Pages 64-65

It is Christmas in the old Regina Coeli prison too. Father Vittorio Trani, the long-serving chaplain, celebrates mass for the inmates in the first rotunda of the ancient Roman Penitentiary Institute.

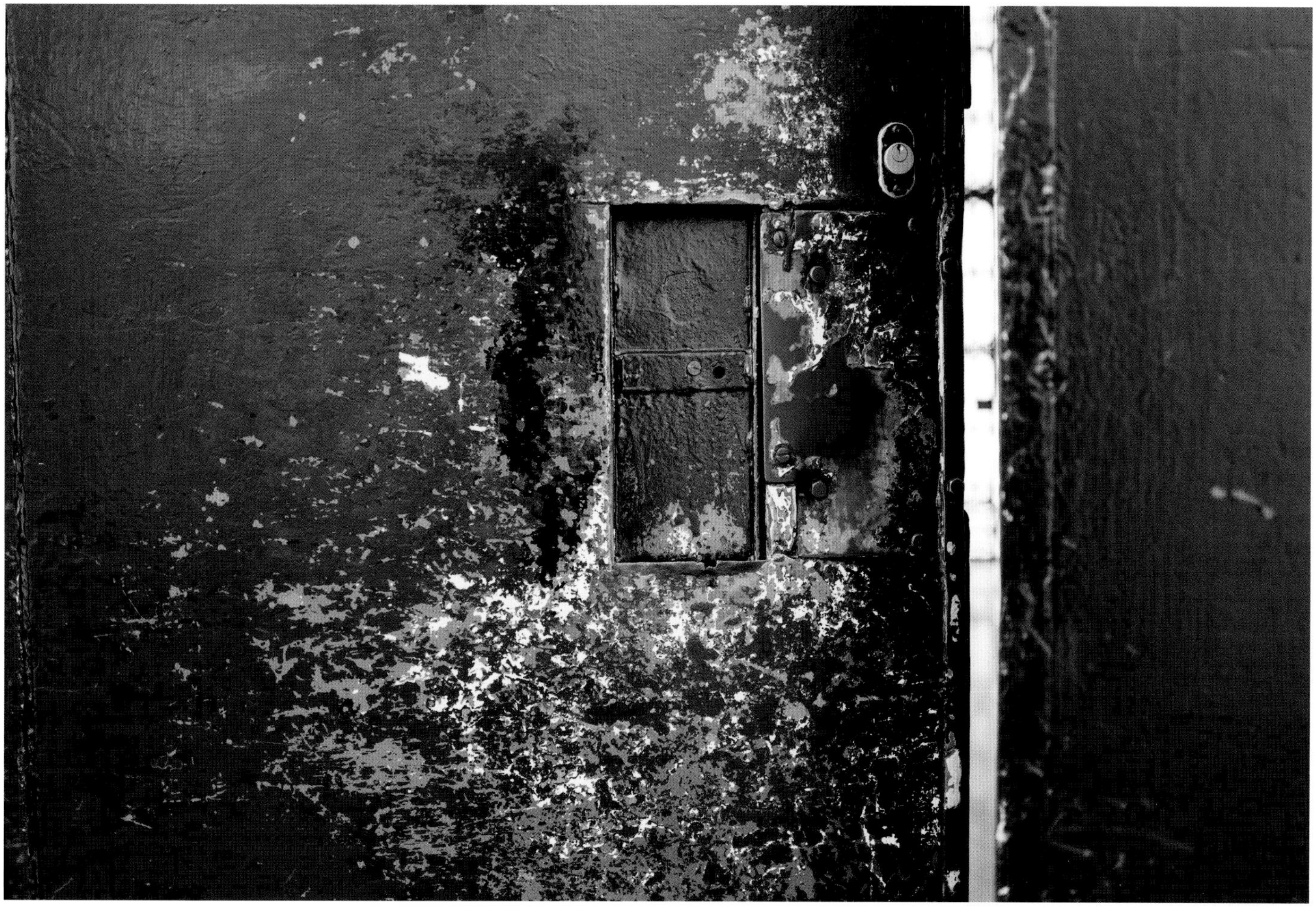

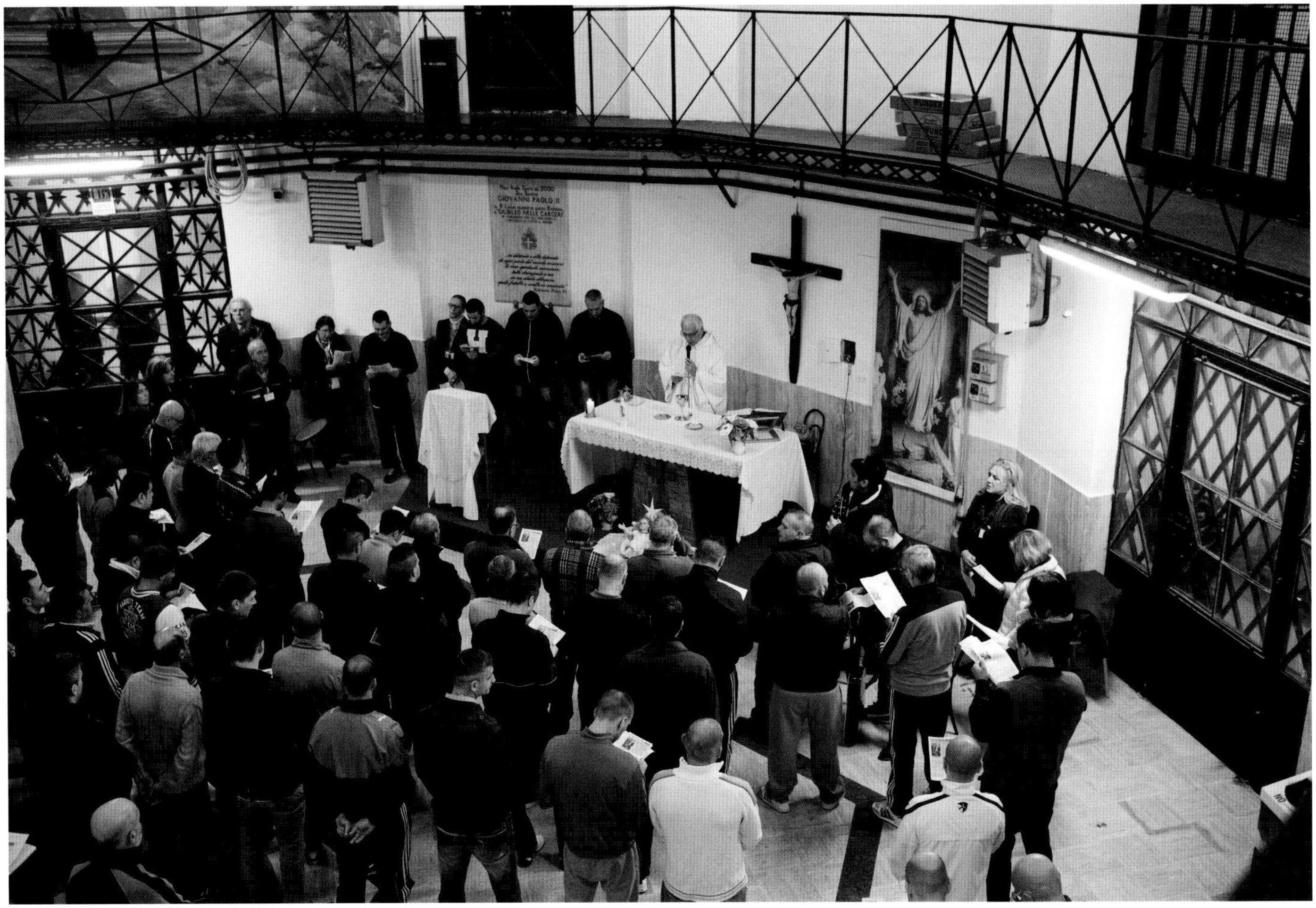
GIOVANNI PAOLO II

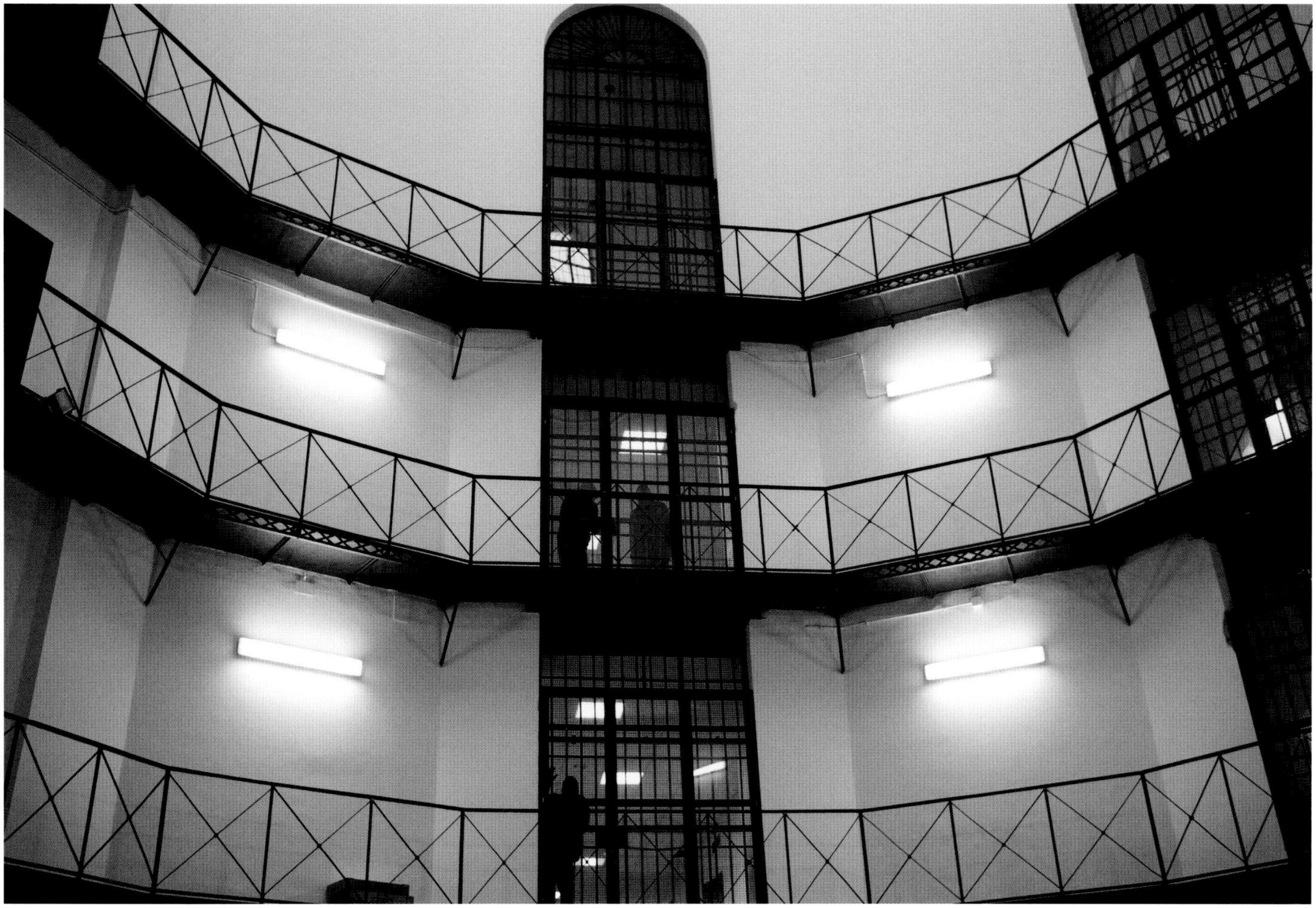

The inmates have prepared a nativity scene for the Christmas celebrations and one of them holds a statue of baby Jesus that he has restored.

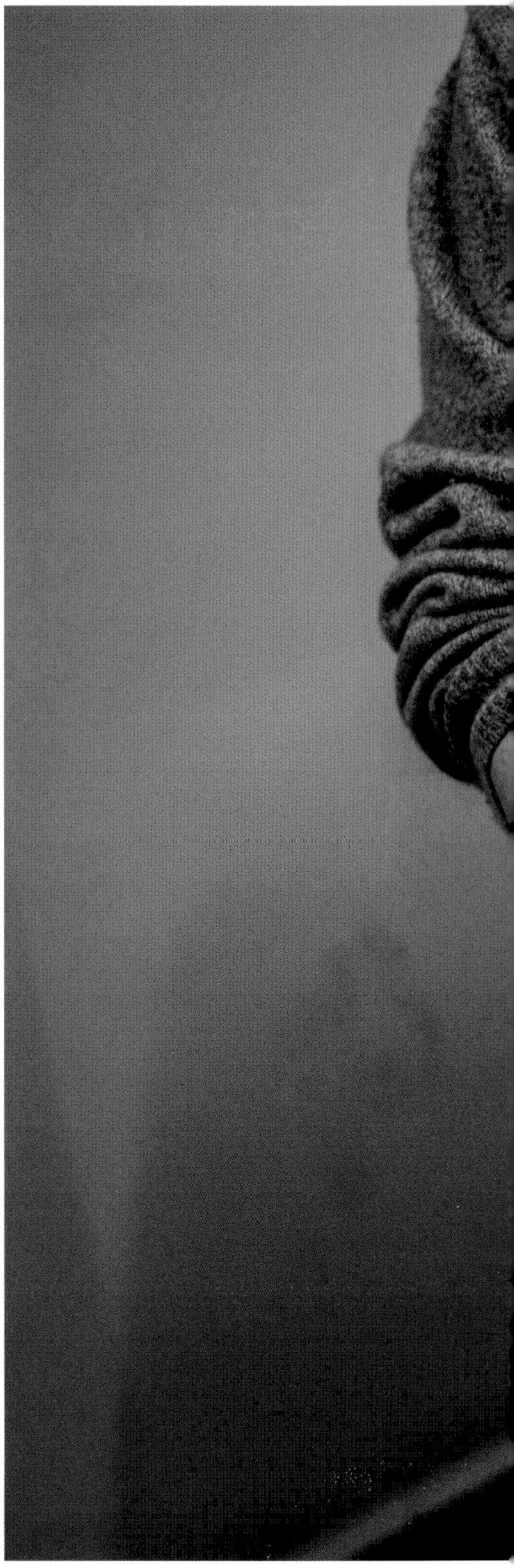

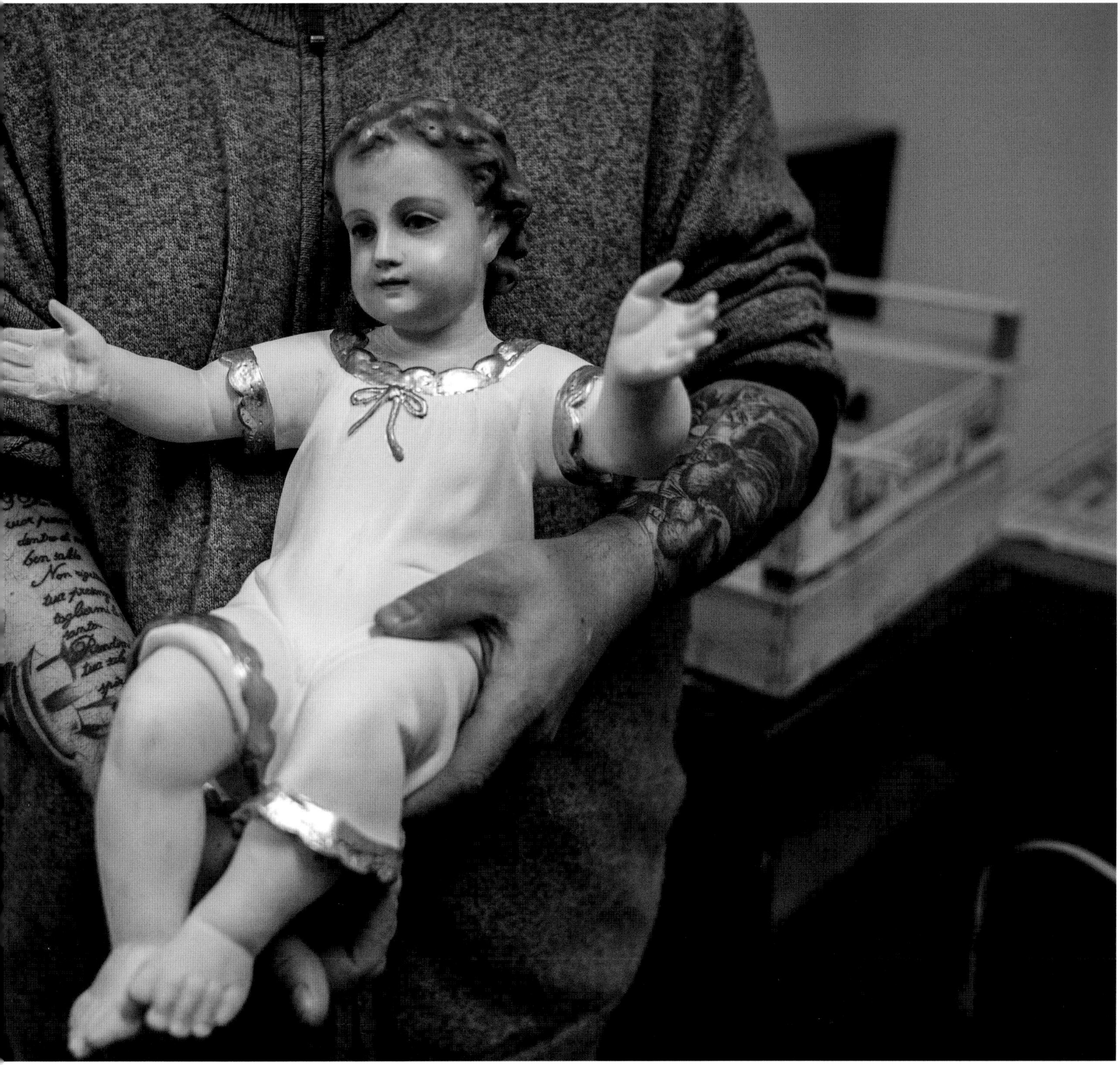

Father Vittorio Trani inaugurated the prison chapel during the Jubilee of Mercy. It was the Holy Thursday before Easter. According to tradition, the ceremony requires the washing of the feet to remember an act by Jesus. The priest knelt to wash and then kiss the feet of an inmate.

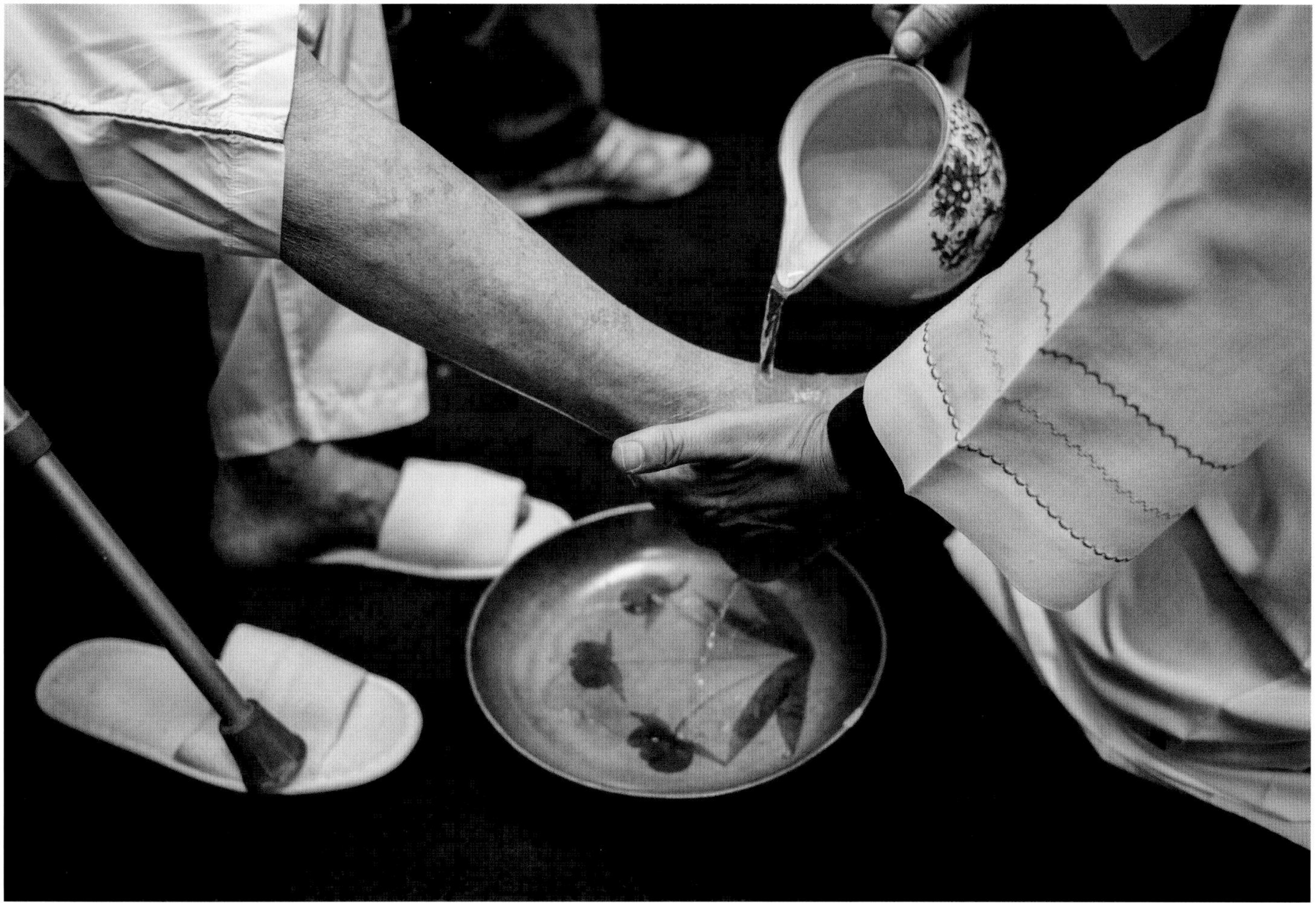

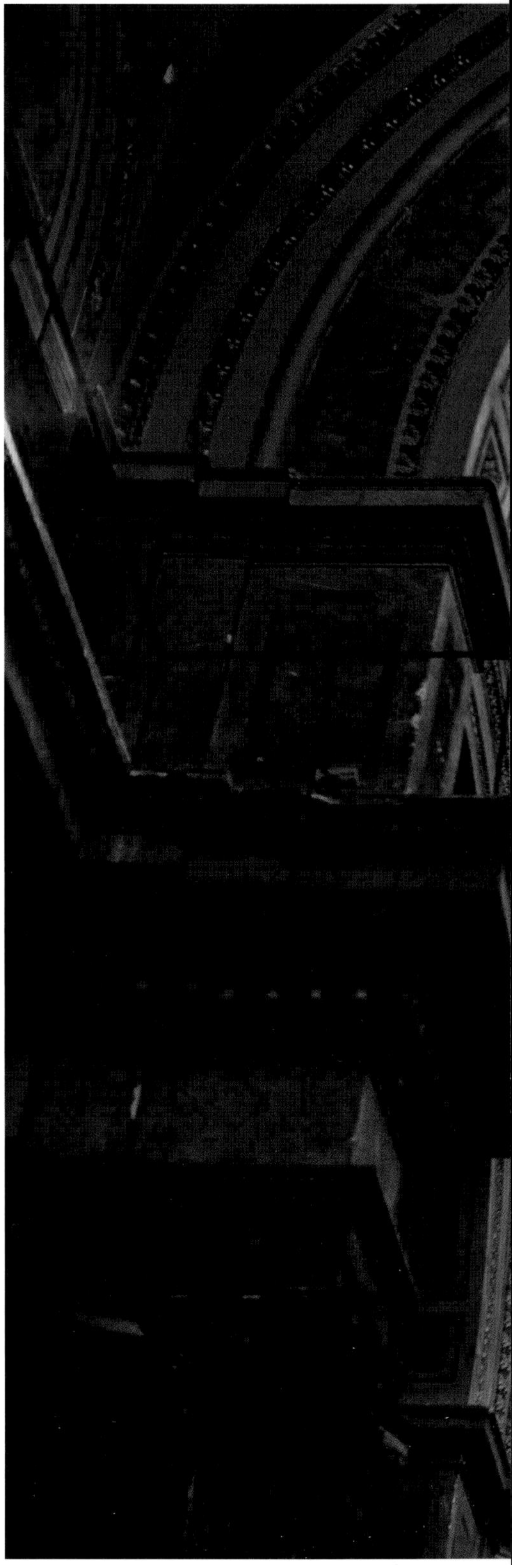

A ray of light pierces the dome of the church of Santa Trinità dei Pellegrini.

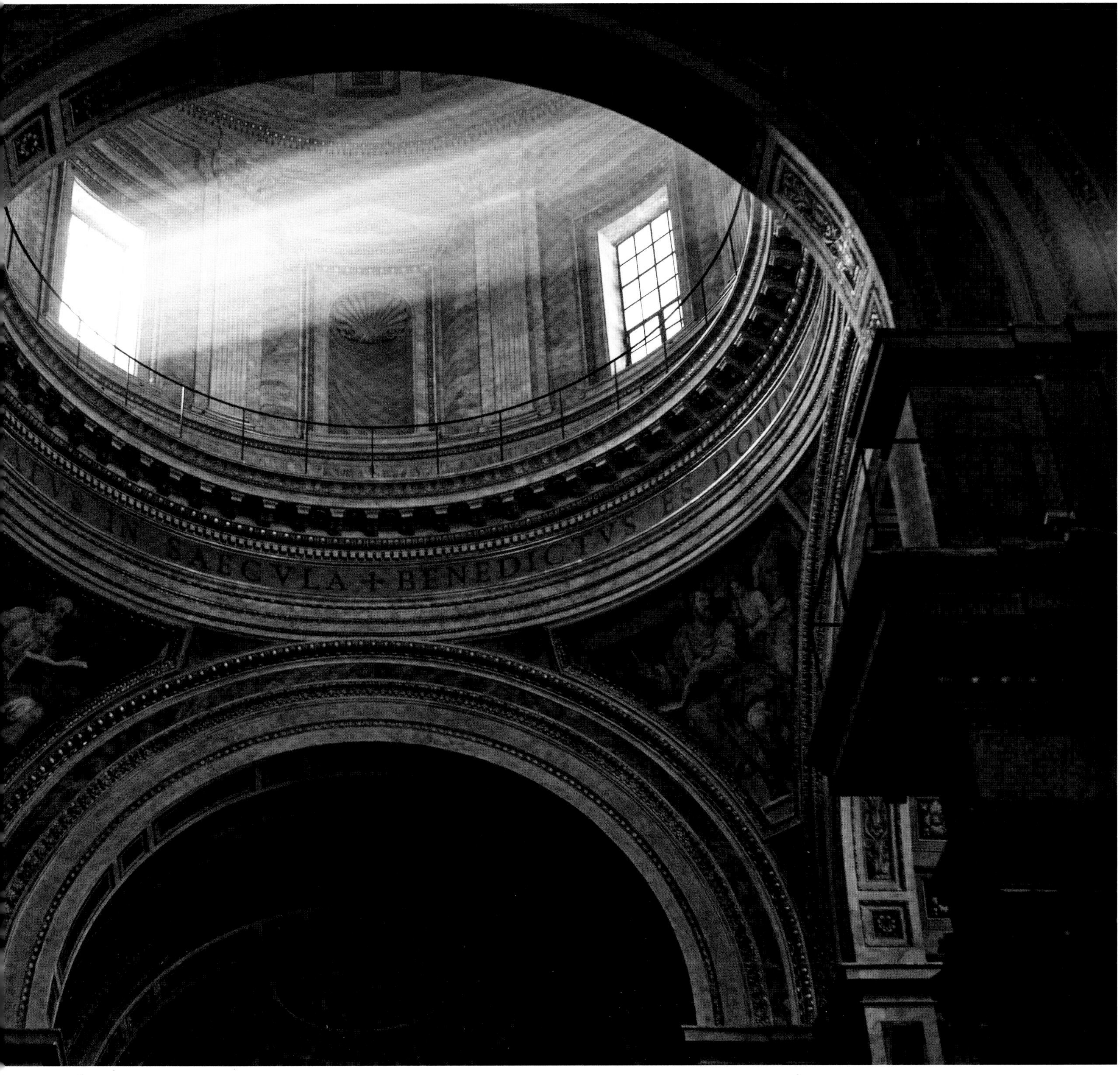
IN SAECVLA BENEDICTVS ES

Since 23 March 2008, the parish has celebrated mass and the sacraments using ancient Roman rites, as declared by Pope Benedict XVI. The ceremonies are extremely well organised, mass is held in Latin and Gregorian chants are sung. Men wear suits and ties and women cover their heads. It offers a glimpse of the old traditional Roman Church.

Pages 74-79

The celebration of Palm Sunday in the parish of Santa Trinità dei Pellegrini is a real event! The faithful follow a procession of clerics and bishops holding the blessed olive branches through the narrow cobbled streets behind the majestic Piazza Farnese. It is a sight from another era: clouds of incense and precious ancient religious vestments.

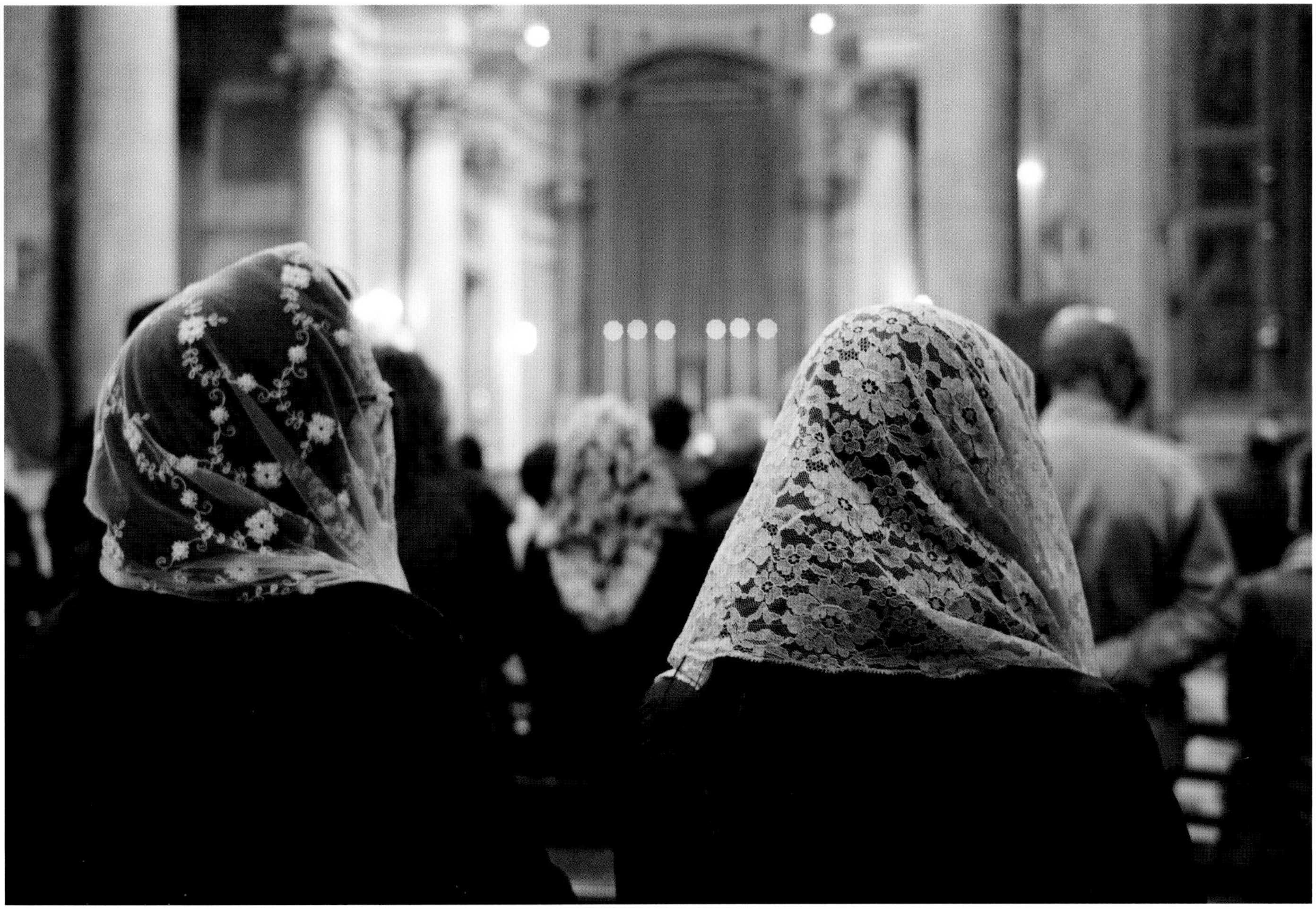

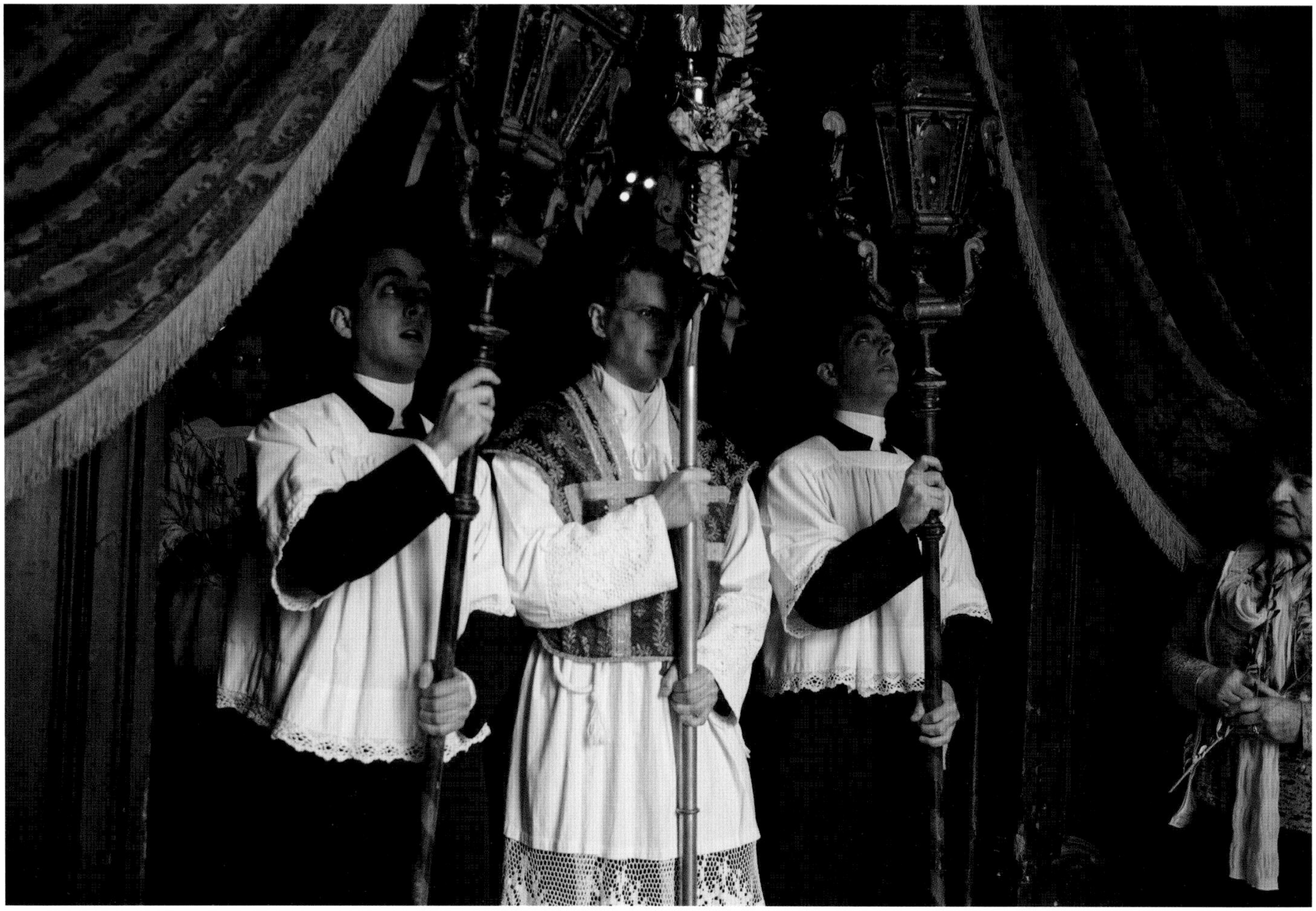

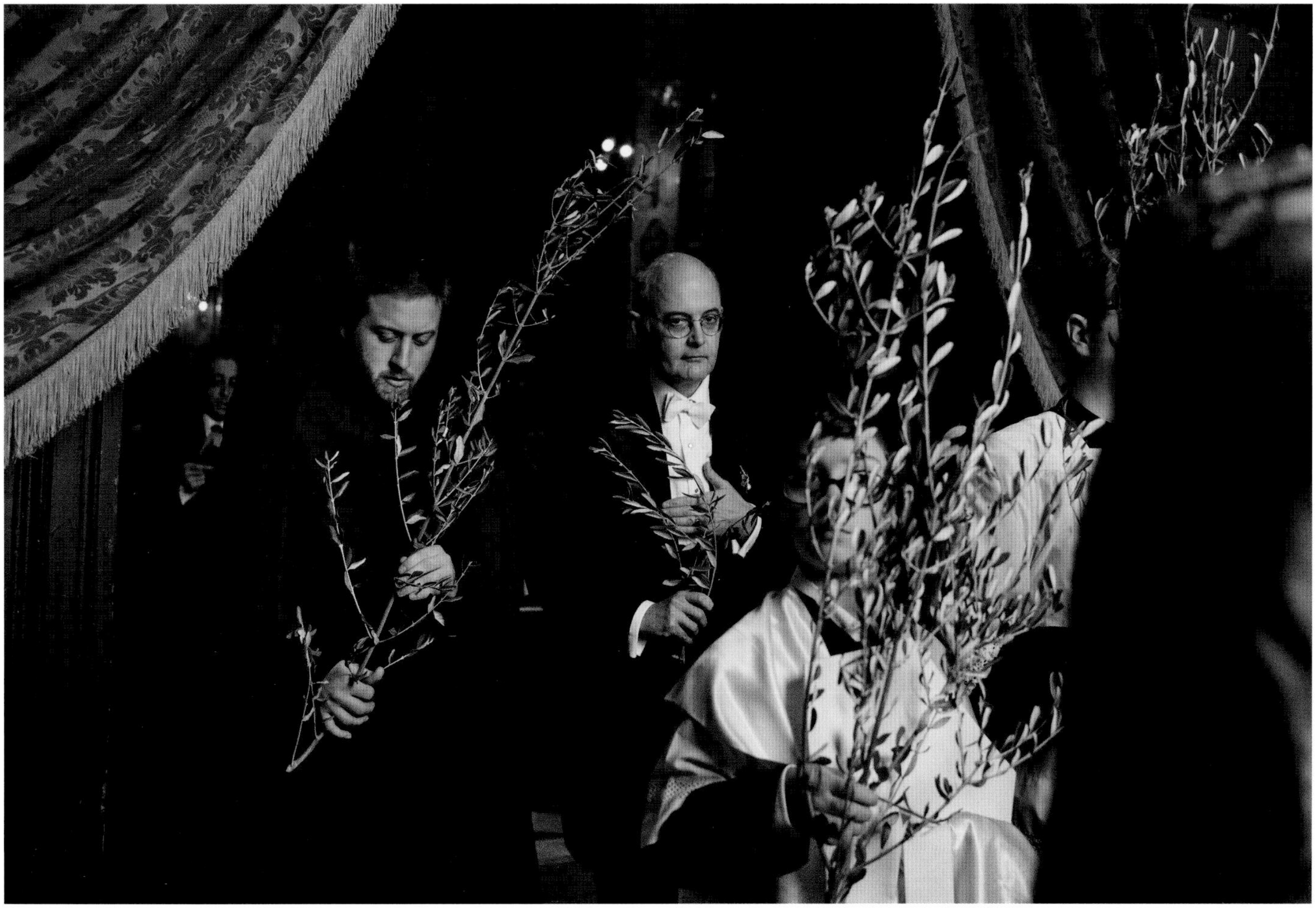

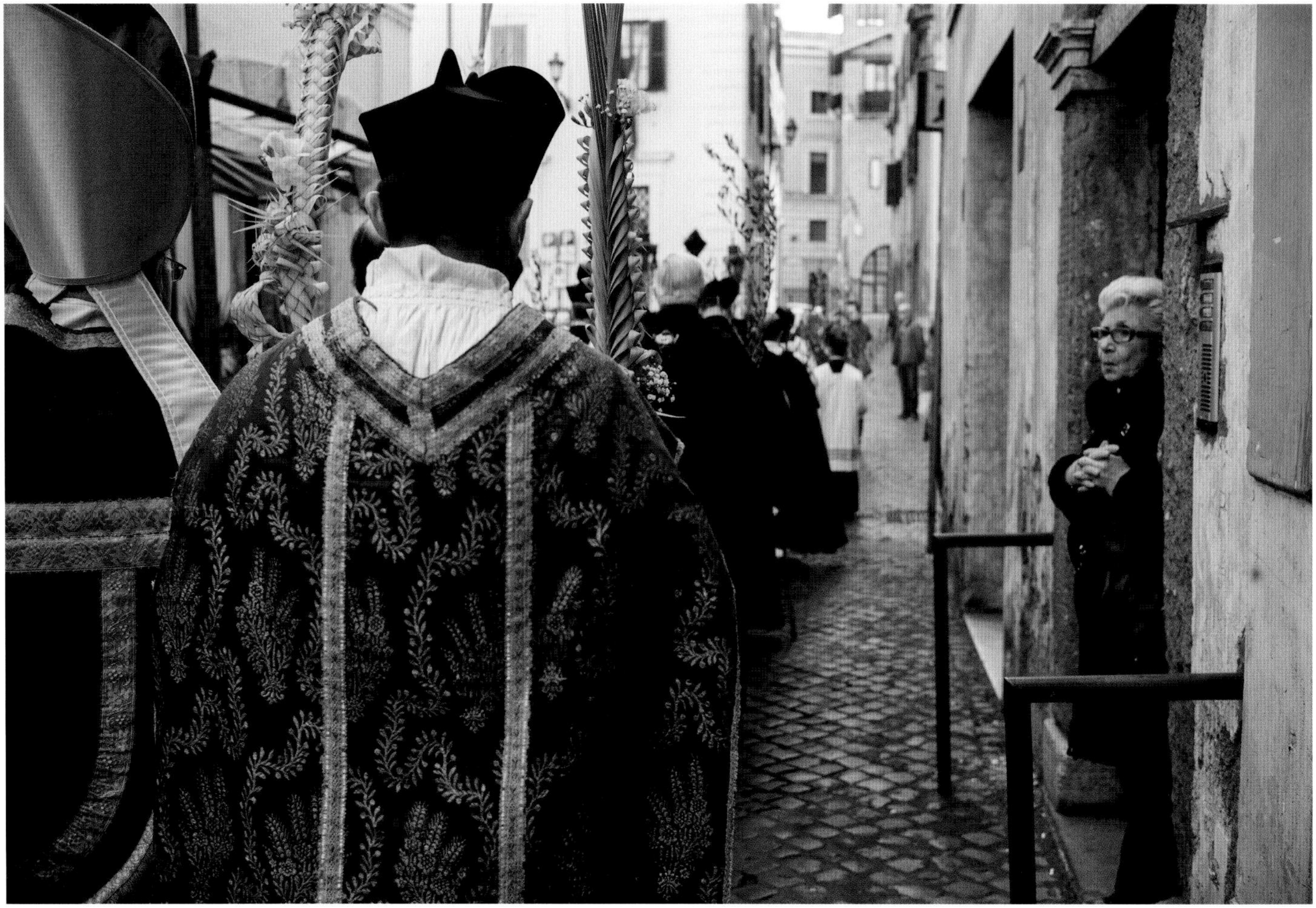

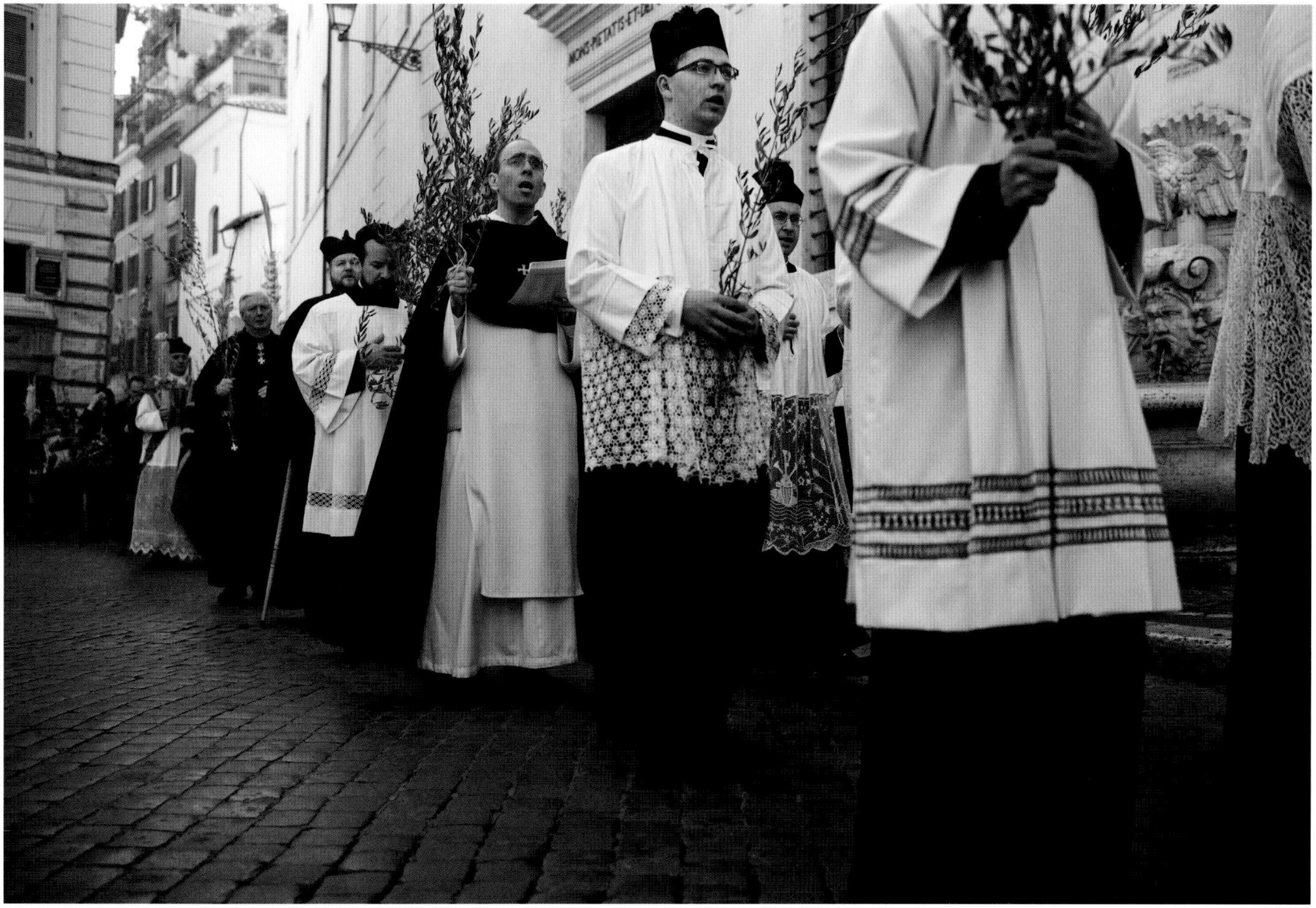

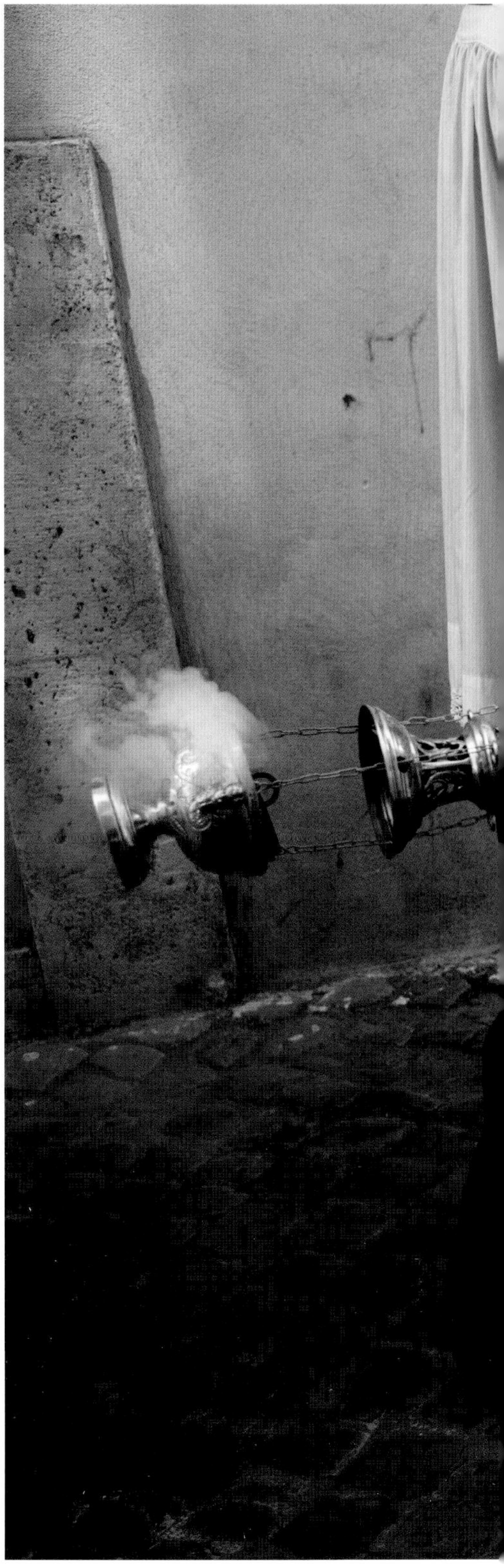

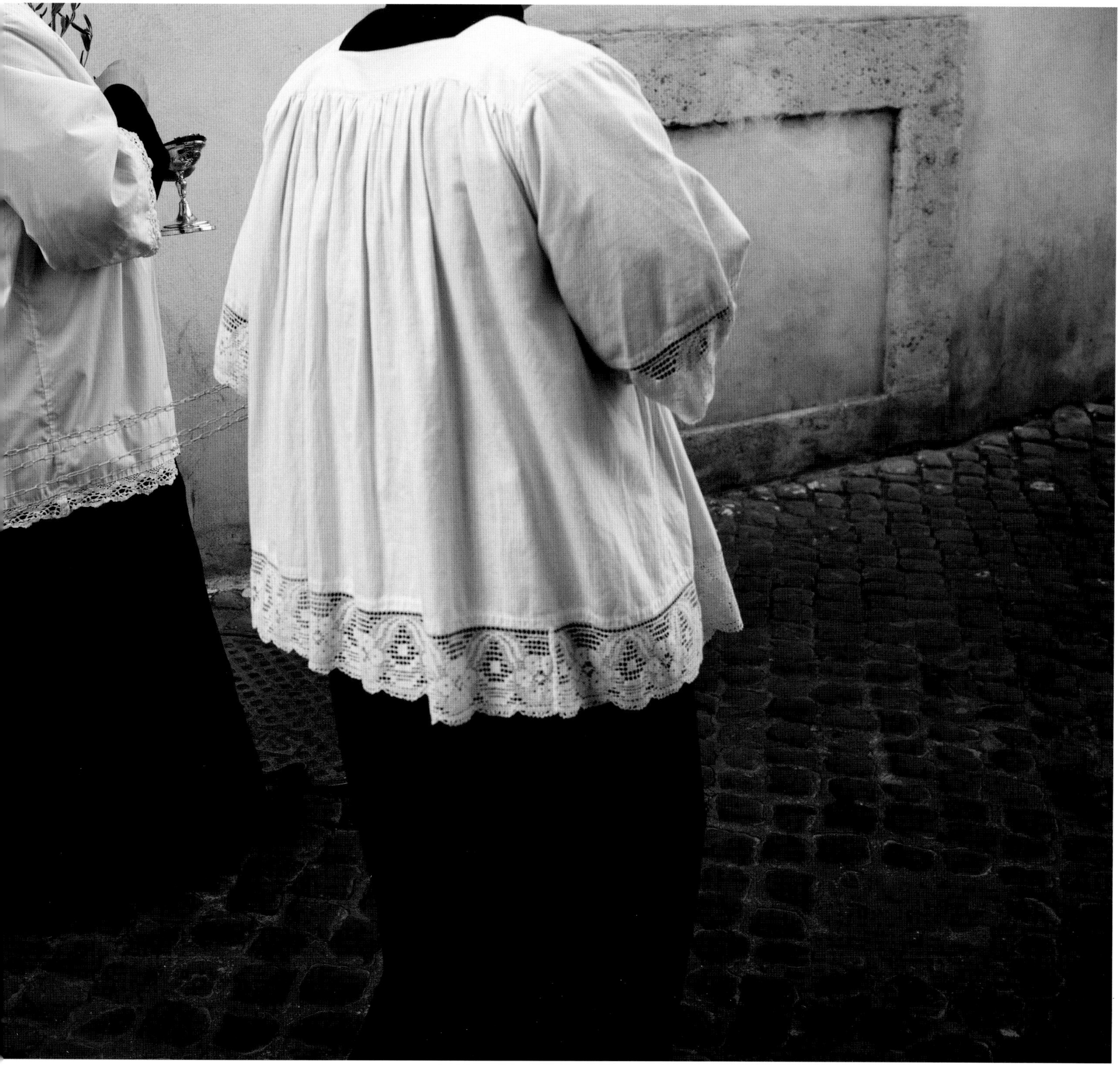

On Good Friday the church celebrates the death of Jesus Christ with the rite of the Via Crucis. Pope Francis took part in the celebration from the Oppian Hill. Behind him and around the Colosseum, historic location for Christian martyrdom, thousands of believers stood with lit candles.

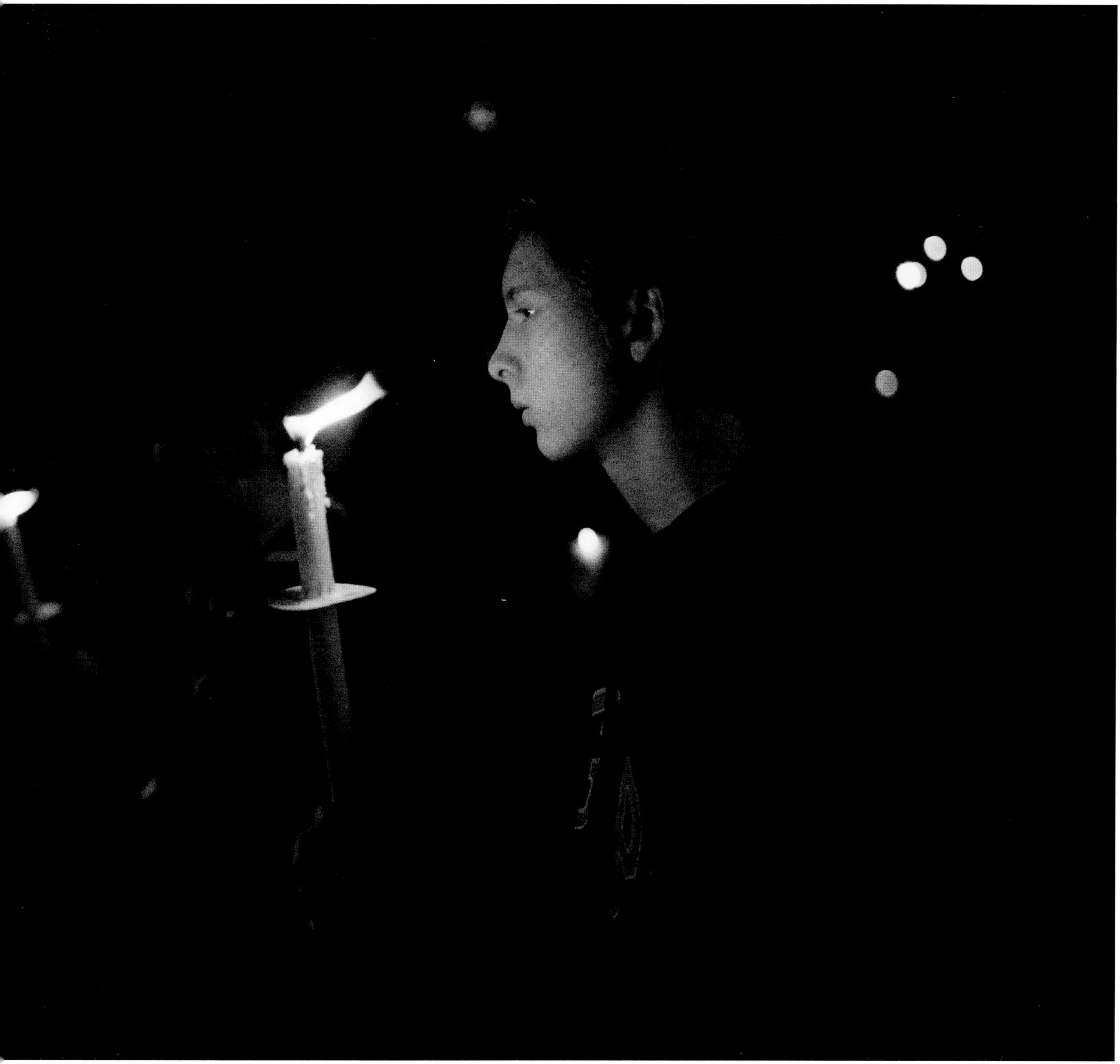

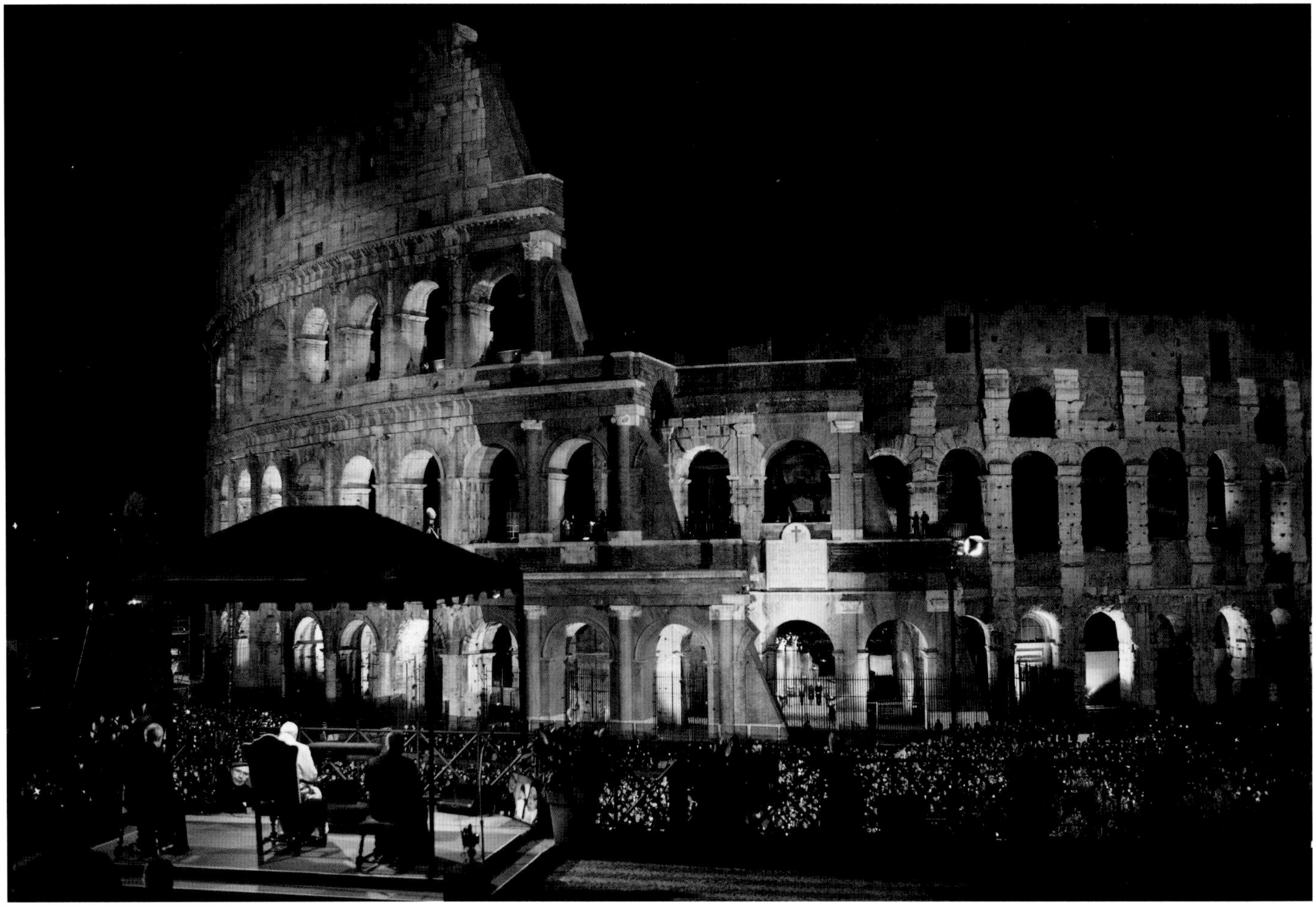

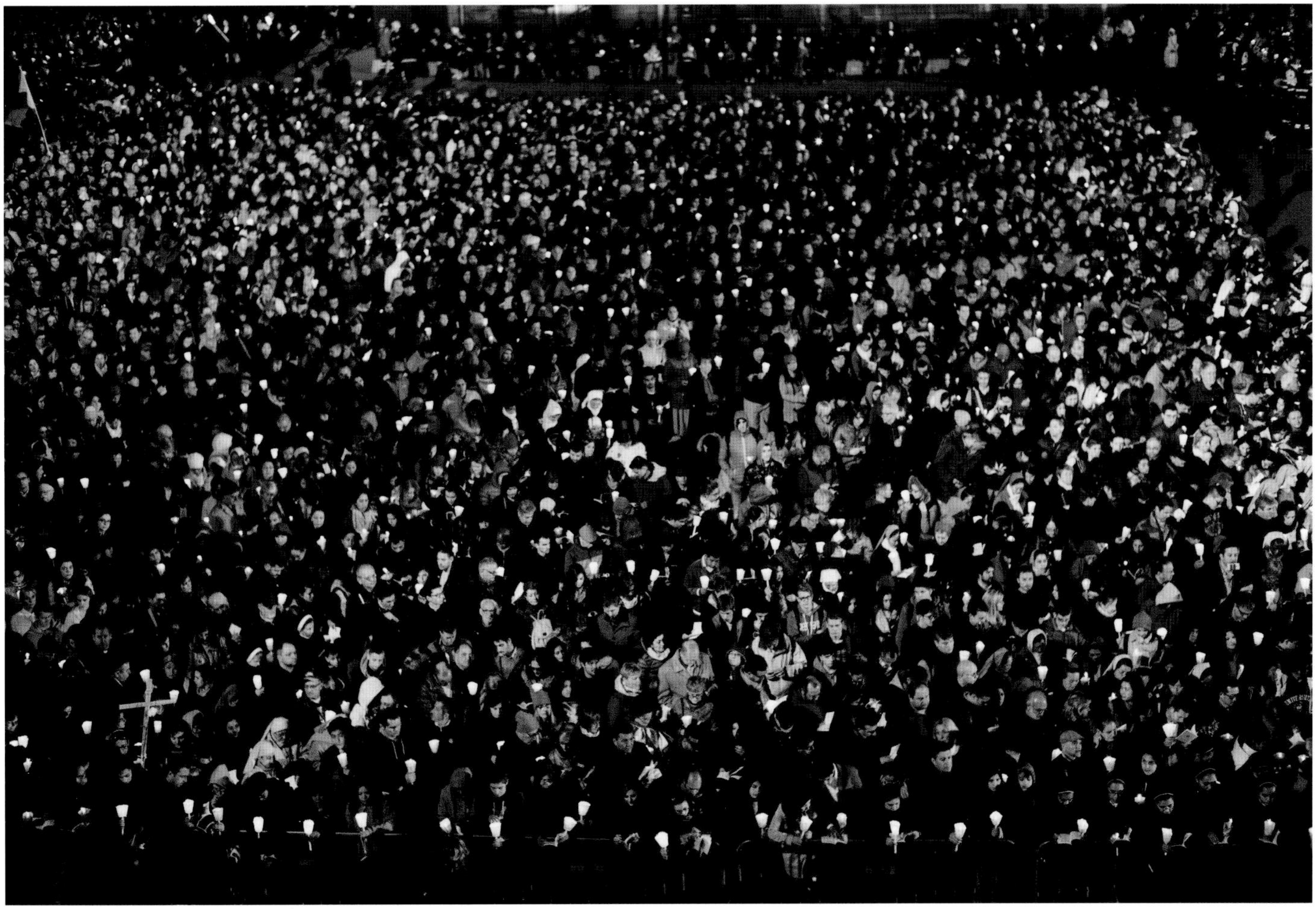

There is something unique to the left of the entrance door to the church of Santa Maria del Popolo: a grating imprisons a skeleton. Beneath is the ironic comment *Neque illic mortuus. Neque Hic vivuus* which means "Neither living here, nor dead there". It is the funerary monument for architect Giovanni Battista Gisleni.

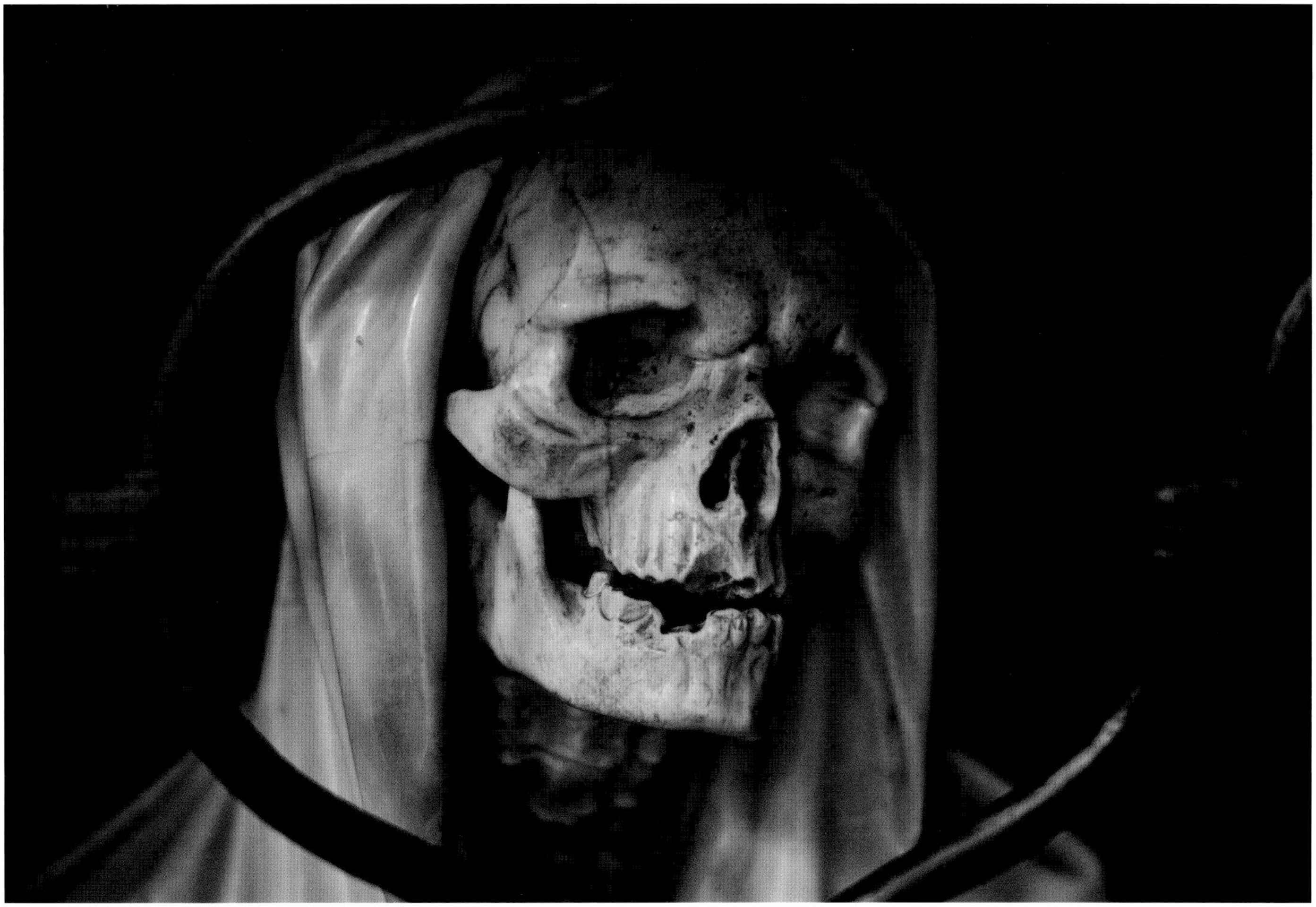

Pope Clement IX wanted ten angels of passion on the bridge of Castel Sant'Angelo. According to the design by Lorenzo Bernini, they were positioned on the parapets of the bridge so as to be admired from below and have the sky as their background.

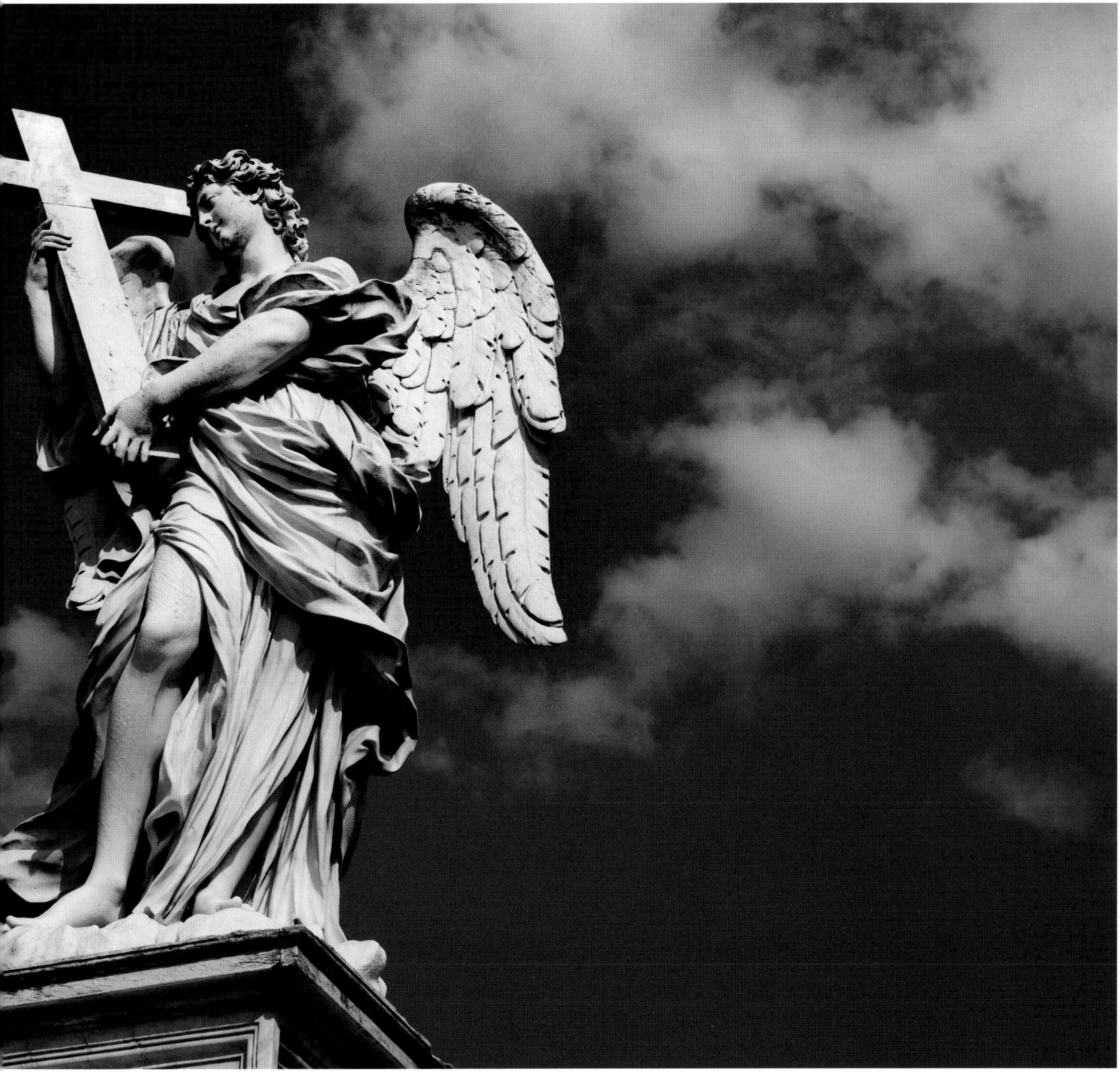

First edition published in 2017

Book design: Alessandra d'Urso, Holger Feroudj and Gerhard Steidl
Tritone separations by Steidl
Production and printing: Steidl, Göttingen

Translation: Victoria Miller
Copy-editing: Monte Packham

Steidl
Düstere Str. 4 / 37073 Göttingen, Germany
Phone +49 551 49 60 60 / Fax +49 551 49 60 649
mail@steidl.de
steidl.de

ISBN 978-3-95829-258-1
Printed in Germany by Steidl